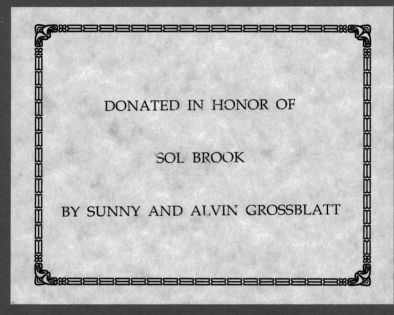

The Most Beautiful Country Towns of Tuscany

JAMES BENTLEY

PHOTOGRAPHS BY ALEX RAMSAY

with 275 color illustrations

Thames & Hudson

HALF-TITLE PAGE
The view into a Tuscan country town: the Arco Senese at
Massa Marittima.

TITLE PAGES
From the town to the Tuscan countryside: the church at
Decimo viewed from San Casciano in Val di Pesa.

OPPOSITE: ABOVE, CENTRE AND BELOW
The variety of Tuscan towns: Castelvecchio, near Pescia;
the west side of Certaldo; the harbour at Porto Ercole.

Designed by Liz Rudderham

First published in hardcover in the United States
of America in 2001 by Thames & Hudson Inc.,
500 Fifth Avenue, New York, New York 10110

© 2001 Thames & Hudson Ltd, London
Text © 2001 Estate of James Bentley
Photographs © 2001 Alex Ramsay

Library of Congress Catalog Card Number
2001086848
ISBN 0-500-51052-0

Printed and bound in Singapore by C. S. Graphics

Contents

Introduction

During my travels and researches for the predecessor and companion volume of the present book, *The Most Beautiful Villages of Tuscany*, it was painfully apparent to me that there were many extraordinary and beautiful places which would have to be left out of that book on the grounds of size and population. The proposal, therefore, to publish a book on the most attractive towns of Tuscany and to cooperate with the photographer Alex Ramsay was welcome indeed; and so, though still against the same backcloth of that harmonious and tranquil countryside of vineyards, olive groves, cornfields, parasol pines and cypresses, this account of those more extensive communities came into being.

The several distinct regions of Tuscany are varied indeed – a variety fully reflected in the characters of its country towns. In the north and north-east are the mountains of the Apuan Alps and the Apennines, where venerable fortified communities cling precariously to the prominences on which they were built for defensive reasons. Further south lies the basin of the Arno, with villages and towns devoted to agriculture and the production of some of the most famous wines of Tuscany. Still further south rise such peaks as Monte Amiata, an extinct volcano and the highest point of the region south of the Arno; the towns there are surrounded by slopes of oak and beech woods, olive groves, cornfields and vineyards. Coastal Tuscany is delicious. One of its most ardent admirers was Charles Dickens, who wrote enthusiastically of 'the free blue sea, with here and there a picturesque felucca gliding slowly on'. Inland, he noted, 'are lofty hills, ravines besprinkled with white cottages, patches of dark olive woods, country churches with their light open towers, and country houses gaily painted.' Here is the land known as the Maremma, stretching from Massa Marittima and Follonica in the north to Orbetello and the Argentario promontory in the south. Now a national park, its towns are renowned centres for tourists attracted by the teeming animal-and bird-life in the forests and along the coastal strip.

The dying light of early evening enlivens the severe façades of the houses of Volterra (opposite) *which confront the strange crumbling ridge of the* Balze. *Further south, the watery pursuits of the spa of Chianciano Terme are neatly symbolized by this fountain in the Piazza Matteotti* (above).

Tuscany's fine and varied cuisine inspires the existence of delightful markets: at Colle di Val d'Elsa (top) and at Chianciano Terme (above). Olives and superb meats (opposite) are other staples of regional dishes.

The fascination of the towns of Tuscany for the inhabitants of more northerly climes is legendary. And part of that fascination is undoubtedly inspired by the cuisine and wines of the area, where certain specialities are associated with particular towns and their surrounding villages. Even a hundred years ago, long before the desire for fine Mediterranean food was widespread, Janet Ross published her classic *Leaves from our Tuscan Kitchen* in recognition of the delights of the local vegetable cookery. Each area has its culinary specialities: *cacciucco*, the spicy fish soup, is naturally associated with the coastal towns; beef comes from the white cattle of the Chiana valley; sausages are made from the wild boar of the Maremma; lentil and bean soups are associated with the towns and villages around Siena; and in the Garfagnana pork with chestnut polenta is especially prized. Tuscan cheeses include *pecorino*, both mild and strong, and the cottage cheese known as *ricotta*. Bread is also celebrated here, and the area around Montecatini Terme claims to produce the finest. And, of course, there is the wine. Impruneta is the start of a Chianti wine route which stretches to Siena; the wines of that region are matched by those of the beautiful Renaissance town of Montepulciano is justly proud of its vineyards, which lie to the south-east of the Chianti region; these produce the famous Vino Nobile di Montepulciano.

The towns described and photographed in this book all share extensively in the wonderful artistic patrimony of Tuscany, from churches and museums filled with fine medieval, Renaissance and Baroque works of art to modern crafts and literature: alabaster at Volterra, flowers at Pesci, and books at Pontrémoli. This is the land of Donatello, Duccio, Giotto, Fra Angelico, Ghirlandaio, Botticelli, the della Robbia family, Michelangelo and Piero della Francesca. Even relatively small towns hold considerable numbers of art treasures: for instance, works by Luca della Robbia and Donatello in Impruneta. Among the many architects and craftsmen who have helped shape these exceptionally beautiful places are Arnolfo di Cambio, Andrea Pisano, Brunelleschi, the Sangallo brothers and

Michelozzo. Their works appear repeatedly in the towns of this book: the Medici villa near Fiesole by Michelozzo; the fortress for the same family at Sansepolcro by Giuliano da Sangallo.

The cultural wealth of the Tuscan Renaissance, however, is only one body of supreme achievement in a long and fascinating history. The mysterious Etruscans, who inhabited the region from the ninth century to the second before the Christian era, developed a remarkable civilization, later partly adopted by the Romans. Both of their legacies are frequently found side by side in Tuscan towns – notably in Fiesole. Indeed, the latter is an especially striking example of the multiple cultural layering which is at the heart of these towns; its Romanesque architecture, for instance, represents another high-mark of architectural achievement. Tuscany was also touched by Byzantium, an influence seen notably in the art of the Sienese painters. Many of these towns enjoyed a great deal of independence until the rise of the cities of Florence and Siena, and even when they fell under the suzerainty of one or the other, their importance continued to be expressed in splendid *palazzi*, often with façades embellished with the carved coats of arms of local notables: the

Every angle of a Tuscan town seems to introduce a new perspective: looking out through the Porta San Felice in Volterra (above)*; resting above the Tuscan landscape on the walls of Fiesole* (right)*. Most Tuscan towns are marked by layers of history expressed in architecture; the Duomo of Chiusi* (opposite) *was begun in the sixth century, rebuilt in the thirteenth, and restored in the nineteenth.*

Palazzo del Podestà at Massa Marittima or the Palazzo Pretorio at Certaldo. And everywhere the influence of the Medici family is visible, as its patronage produced a uniquely rich body of art and architecture, marking these towns with an indelible imprint. So strong are the presences of medieval times and the Renaissance that we tend to think of Tuscan towns almost entirely in terms of the styles of those periods; yet, notably in the spa towns, are delightful twentieth-century exercises in neo-Renaissance, neo-Baroque and Art Deco. See, for instance, the elegant thermal establishments and hotels of Montecatini Terme, the town where Giuseppe Verdi composed the last act of *Otello*.

The country towns described and photographed in this book exemplify the remarkable variety of this part of Italy; they also embody its exceptional cultural heritage, from the Etruscan and Romanesque north, to the walled communities of the centre, to the thermal centres and coastal resorts in the south. Together, they constitute a uniquely beautiful and rewarding ensemble.

NORTHERN TUSCANY

Valleys and their rivers define and shape northern Tuscany and therefore the siting of its towns. 'There are so many little deep valleys', noted D.H.Lawrence, 'with streams that seem to go their own little way entirely....'. Some of the towns in this area, like Sansepolcro and Pontrémoli, are located on river banks, while others, like Barga, have commanding views of river valleys from some prominence. Here, the presence of the Etruscans is often felt; their walls still circle the amphitheatre of Fiesole, a town which they probably founded. Medieval architecture is abundantly represented: Romanesque churches abound, like Barga's cathedral of San Cristofano; the Gothic style is displayed in all its splendour in Pescia. This is also the land of Renaissance and Baroque villas, to which the leading aristocratic families of the region would repair to seek rural peace away from the city crowds. And this is Chianti country.

Close to Pescia lies the compact hill-town of Castelvecchio (opposite). *It is especially renowned for its Romanesque church of San Tommaso.*

Barga

TODAY, THE MODERN PART OF THIS fortified town sits at the foot of the hill on which it was founded. The steep streets of the old part, taxing to the legs of visitors and locals alike, meander around the upper reaches of the prominence which dominates the wooded valley of the Serchio half-a-dozen kilometres north-west of Bagni di Lucca in the region known as the Garfagnana. From here the views over the river valley are especially magnificent. Because of its site and therefore its strategic importance, the cities of Lucca, Florence and Pisa strove for power over the town in the Middle Ages, with Florence eventually achieving dominance in 1341.

One of the town's greatest architectural treasures is its splendid Romanesque cathedral. For the most part

Rising above the blind arcades of the main church, the battlemented tower of the cathedral dominates Barga (above). In typical Romanesque fashion, the windows of the tower begin with two-light groupings, above which are three lights. Rising above the town, the cathedral offers breathtaking views of the surrounding mountains (opposite); its west door opens here on to the Pannia della Croce and the Pannia Secca. Indeed, the whole town is cradled by mountains (overleaf).

Barga is remarkable for its wealth of sculpted stone decoration: a coat of arms above a doorway in the patrician Via del Pretorio (opposite); details of the cathedral (this page). Stylized plants and a wine harvest embellish the arch and architrave of the cathedral door (above). It is also guarded by lions which occur again as supports of the marble pulpit inside the cathedral (left), reminders of St. Peter's claim that, outside the sanctuary of the church, the devil is like a roaring lion.

this dates from the twelfth century, though it was founded in the ninth and later embellished in the thirteenth; chapels were added in the sixteenth and eighteenth centuries. It was damaged by an earthquake in 1920, but has now been beautifully restored. The severe façade, flanked by a crenellated campanile, has the stern beauty of Lombardic Romanesque architecture, decorated with sculpted human beings and fabulous animals. Note the scene of a grape harvest above the main entrance. Inside is a fresco of *St. Christopher*, painted in the eighteenth century by Stefano Tofanelli. Nearby is a fourteenth-century fresco of *St. Lucy*. The pulpit, the magnificent work of the thirteenth-century Como sculptor Guido Bigorelli, rises on pink marble columns from the figures of an old bearded man and two lions. Other reliefs on the pulpit show the prophet *Isaiah*, the *Annunciation*, the *Birth of Jesus* and the *Adoration of the Magi*. Works by members of the della Robbia family adorn the chapel of the Holy Sacrament. In the apse is a magnificent polychrome statue in wood

of the cathedral's patron saint, sculpted in the twelfth century. To the right of the high altar is a terracotta piece showing the *Virgin Mary with Saints Sebastian and Roch*. To the left of the same altar is a fifteenth-century painted crucifix and a contemporary view of Barga in a sixteenth-century painting of *St. Joseph*.

Standing out above the intriguing network of streets which constitute the old town, the cathedral is neighbour to the Palazzo Pretorio, with its fourteenth-century *loggetta*, decorated with coats of arms. Today, the building houses a permanent exhibition of local prehistory.

The fourteenth-century church of San Francesco is well worth a visit, especially for the three altars which incorporate work by the della Robbia family: a *Nativity*, *St. Francis with the Stigmata*, and the *Assumption of the Virgin Mary*.

*S*plendid interiors abound in and around Barga: the Baroque church at Tiglio Alto, east of the town (opposite); the ceiling of San Giusto (right); the auditorium of the Teatro dell' Accademia (below).

*N*arrow streets and irregular rooftops characterize many a Tuscan town, creating plays of light and shade. In quiet lanes and corners, daily life goes on: in the Via di Mezzo (left); a shopkeeper in the Piazza del Comune (below); and beyond the houses of the main town stretch the terraces of the surrounding landscape (opposite).

Bibbiena

In one of the squares of Bibbiena stands the twelfth-century church of Santi Ippolito e Donato, dedicated in part to the patron saint of this engaging hill and market town. Close by, a terrace yields superb panoramic views of this part of the upper valley of the Arno, including the villages of Poppi and Camaldoli. Tree-clad mountains surround the town, the principal community in the region known as the Casentino. It enters recorded history only in the tenth century A.D., but there is speculation that its name is in fact derived from an Etruscan family named Vibia, and thus the town may have a very long pedigree.

Now famous for its salami, Bibbiena's past would in any case have guaranteed its long-lasting distinction.

Viewed from a distance across fields of sunflowers (right), Bibbiena dominates the upper valley of the Arno. Within it, the visitor is guaranteed a constant succession of the grand and the intimate, like this table set for conviviality in a courtyard off the Via Cappucci (below).

The ancient stones of the Porta dei Fabbri incorporate a shrine (opposite). More examples of the fine detailing of Bibbiena (this page) are these balconies on the Piazza Roma, the juxtaposition of modern newspapers with old stonework, and an entertaining wall-fountain in the Piazza Matteotti.

In the fifteenth century the town was the birthplace of Bernardo Dovizi, who entered the church, became a cardinal, taking the name of the town, and secretary to Pope Leo X. In the early sixteenth century he commissioned the building of the Palazzo Dovizi – certainly the finest of several splendid *palazzi* in Bibbiena – in a beautiful Tuscan rustic style. He was also the patron of Raphael and in his own right an author, writing the first comedy in Italian theatre in 1513.

His palace stands in the Via Dovizi, opposite the fifteenth-century church of San Lorenzo. Triple-naved, this church contains some magnificent terracottas by the della Robbia family. More treasures can be found in Santi Ippolito e Donato, which stands in the Piazza Tarlati: late-medieval frescoes, a triptych by Bicci di Lorenzo in 1435 and above all a painting of the *Madonna and Child with Angels* by Arcangelo di Cola da Camerino. The sixteenth-century Palazzo Comunale is another outstanding building.

A rewarding excursion from Bibbiena is to visit the convent (still in use) which St. Francis of Assisi founded at La Verna. Lying east of Bibbiena in a forest of fir and beech trees, this was the spot where on 14 September 1224 the saint received the stigmata. Here,

along with the saint's cell, are numerous churches: the Capella delle Stimmate, built in 1263 on the spot where the miracle happened, with a *Crucifixion* by Andrea della Robbia and Renaissance stalls; the church of Santa Maria degli Angeli, founded in 1216, again with della Robbia masterpieces and housing the sanctuary museum; and the fourteenth- and fifteenth-century convent church, with an *Annunciation* and a *Nativity* by Andrea della Robbia. One kilometre north-east of Bibbiena lies the church of Santa Maria del Sasso, attached to a Dominican monastery. It contains frescoed ex-votos, a fifteenth-century fresco of the *Virgin Mary and the Infant Jesus* by Bicci di Lorenzo and a late-fifteenth century tabernacle by Bartolomeo Bozzolino.

*T*wo notable religious communities are located close to Bibbiena: the monastery of La Verna (top), *founded by St. Francis, and Santa Maria del Sasso* (above *and* right).

*B*ibbiena and its region are exceptionally rich in ecclesiastical art, including this twelfth-century Madonna Enthroned (above) *in the Romanesque church of Santi Ippolito e Donato. Its simplicity contrasts starkly with the opulence of the interior of the Oratorio di San Francesco (right).*

Fiesole

THE VIEW FROM THIS HILL-TOWN is one of the most remarkable in the whole of Tuscany, revealing Florence and the Arno valley. Fiesole, indeed, long outshone its now much larger neighbour, deriving its importance from a position astride one of the major trade routes of Italy and, as *Faesulae*, membership of an ancient federation of powerful city-states. Probably founded by the Etruscans in the sixth century B.C.,

In the past, Fiesole dominated Florence politically and economically; now its dominance is purely geographical (above left).

F *iesole at sunrise (above) reveals the magnificent site of the town on a wooded hill, punctuated by cypresses and the battlemented tower of San Romolo.*

charming and exquisite Fiesole has had its praises sung by many, including Lamartine and Shelley. The Florentines began to wage sporadic war on the hill-town in the eleventh century, but Fiesole held out until 1125. Later, the Florentines began to care for the town; they rebuilt the former cathedral in 1464. In 1458 Cosimo the Elder commissioned Michelozzo to build the Villa Medici on the way from Fiesole to San Domenico.

The Medici also ordered the rebuilding of Fiesole's former cathedral at Badia Fiesolana. San Domenico's fifteenth-century church, where Fra Angelico was first ordained, was enlarged in the seventeenth century. A *Madonna and Angels* and a *Crucifixion* by the painter can be found there.

The legacy of the Etruscans is still highly visible in parts of the main town. Their walls partly protect an

The Badia Fiesolana (above) was the cathedral of Fiesole until 1028. It was rebuilt in the mid fifteenth century on the orders of the Medici, but the white and green marble façade of the older, Romanesque church was retained. Inside is a fresco of The Annunciation by Raffaellino del Garbo (detail, far left). One of the treasures of the present cathedral is a panel (left) carved for the tomb of Bishop Leonardo Salutati by Mino da Fiesole. The church of San Domenico stands just outside Fiesole; its eighteenth-century ceiling (opposite) by Matteo Bonecchi, Rinaldo Botti and Lorenzo del Moro celebrates the glory of the saint.

amphitheatre which the Romans built in the first century B.C.; quite a high proportion of the some three thousand seats still survive. Piazza Mino da Fiesole, named after the fifteenth-century sculptor who came from the town, occupies the site of the old Roman forum. More vestiges of the Roman occupation include columns in the church of Sant' Alessandro.

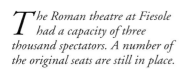*he Roman theatre at Fiesole had a capacity of three thousand spectators. A number of the original seats are still in place.*

Saints adorn the ceiling of the Salutati chapel in the cathedral (below left). *The main altarpiece there is a masterpiece of* c.1440 *by Bicci di Lorenzo* (below right). *Outside, the cathedral's campanile* (opposite) *has a defensive aspect.*

Around Piazza Mino da Fiesole cluster the cathedral of San Romolo, the episcopal palace, the fourteenth- and fifteenth-century Palazzo Pretorio, and the oratory of Santa Maria Primerana, whose porch dates from the late sixteenth century and is home to frescoes from the school of Giotto and terracotta decorations. In the centre of the *piazza* is an equestrian statue, commemorating a meeting of Garibaldi and King Vittorio Emanuele II. Over the main entrance of the cathedral,

consecrated in 1030 and subsequently much restored, is an effigy of its patron, St. Romulus, the work of Giovanni della Robbia. The campanile of 1213 is battlemented. Inside, the magnificent tomb of Bishop Leonardo Salutati, who died in 1456, was carved by Mino da Fiesole and placed in the Capella Salutati; his work can also be seen in the altar frontal, which takes the form of the *Virgin Mary in Adoration with the Saints*. The columns of the crypt are crowned by

Secular and ecclesiastical in Fiesole: the church of Santa Maria Primavera stands next to the Palazzo Comunale (opposite) at the upper end of the Piazza Mino da Fiesole. Other treasures of religious art of the town include another Annunciation *by Raffaellino del Garbo (detail, below left) in the church of San Francesco and frescoes in the Badia Fiesolana (detail, below right). A reminder, though, of Fiesole's former political masters is this interior of a pavilion in the gardens of the Villa Medici (right).*

ancient capitals; the font, altar and accompanying frescoes are all fifteenth-century. The Bishop's mitre and reliquary bust are preserved in the sacristy.

Another superb view of Florence is available from the public gardens which lie next to the fourteenth-century friary of San Francesco. The church has exquisite, tiny cloisters; inside, there is a fifteenth-century fresco depicting its patron.

Impruneta

The cloisters of the collegiate church of Santa Maria dell' Impruneta (below), complete with fountain and wells, provide a peaceful contrast to the external face of the same church (opposite).

SET ON A PLATEAU JUST SOUTH OF Florence and at the northern tip of Chianti country, Impruneta overlooks the valleys of the Greve and the Ema rivers. Its agricultural traditions are commemorated each year in mid-October in the Fiera di San Luca, the cattle fair of St. Luke (whose symbol is a bull). Until recent times the fair was one of the most important in Europe for the trading of mules and horses. Indeed, it was so famous in the past that the Venetian painter Domenico

Tiepolo went there several times to record it, and Jacques Callot, the engraver, made a series of engravings of the town in 1620. Impruneta is also famed for the production of high-quality tiles and bricks in the local kilns.

The most attractive feature of the town, perhaps, is the Basilica di Santa Maria dell'Impruneta which graces the delightfully arcaded main square. Founded in the eleventh century, rebuilt in the fifteenth, it still

retains a high thirteenth-century campanile and a façade created in the sixteenth. Extensively damaged by bombing in 1944, the body of the church has been restored to match its fifteenth-century Renaissance reconstruction, the work of Antonio degli Agli, and the church porch to its design by Gherardo da Silvani in the early seventeenth century. The oldest part of the church is the crypt, which dates from the eleventh century. A fourteenth-century polyptych by Pietro

The human faces of Impruneta: a massive urn provides convenient shade outside the basilica of Santa Maria (below); and life of the twenty-first century goes on beneath the ancient north wall and doorway of the same church (opposite).

*I mpruneta's market takes place
in the Piazza Buondelmonti
(left). The town is especially notable
for its terracotta workshops (below).
The basilica (opposite) houses a
number of masterpieces in terracotta
by Luca della Robbia.
Its elegant portico, a favourite
meeting-place, was designed by
Gherardo Silvani in 1634.*

Nelli embellishes the high altar. In the mid fifteenth century the Florentine Michelozzo designed two side chapels, one of which contains the famous painting of the *Virgin Mary*, allegedly the work of St. Luke the Evangelist. Legend has it that the portrait was brought to Impruneta by St. Romulus who, fearing for its safety, buried it. When the townsfolk later decided to build a church, they agreed they should site it at the place where the oxen bearing the building stone first knelt down. And when the good folk of Impruneta started to dig the foundations there, they discovered the portrait.

The Museo del Tesoro (Treasury) houses a fine display of vestments, choir books and splendid church silver, including a cross by Lorenzo Ghiberti from the second decade of the fifteenth century. There is also a depiction from the workshop of Donatello of the discovery of St. Luke's picture of the Madonna.

An elaborate tempietto *in the basilica houses the celebrated portrait of the Madonna of Impruneta* (opposite)*; less ornate, but certainly elegant, are the cathedral cloisters* (right).

Montecatini Terme

Now one of the largest spas in Italy and once popular with the Romans, Montecatini Terme lies west of Pistoia on the road from Lucca to Florence. It enjoyed a revival during the fourteenth century and really began to flourish in the late eighteenth century under the patronage of Grand Duke Leopoldo II. Later, in the nineteeth century, the spa became a favourite health resort of the European aristocracy. The Leopoldine thermal establishment was constructed in 1775 (and rebuilt in 1926); other celebrated establishments here are the Tettuccio and the Excelsior. Today, the new town's Parco delle Terme has five principal thermal establishments, their extraordinarily rich sulphur and soda springs valued for curing skin and liver disorders.

Many of the buildings which surround the main park are delightful examples of early twentieth-century

Overview and detail of this famous spa town: Montecatini Alto on its hill (left); *and a carving on a shop front* (below).

architecture; the colonnaded Stabilimento Tettuccio, for instance, famous for its café, was built in 1927 in a neo-Renaissance style. Apart from a ruined medieval fortress, the spa town of Montecatini is mainly modern; the Palazzo Comunale dates from 1919 and the church of Santa Maria Assunta from 1962.

Much more ancient is Montecatini Alto (also known as Montecatini Val di Nievole) which has the successive generations of architecture we normally associate with a Tuscan town. The Romanesque church of San Pietro Apostolo has fourteenth-century frescoes; a museum of religious art contains medieval and Renaissance paintings. It lies some distance above the town, from where it is served by a funicular railway. Once of great strategic importance, in the Middle Ages Montecatini Alto was the centre of the conflict between Guelphs and Ghibellines. In medieval Italy and Germany, the Guelphs supported the Popes, while the Ghibellines formed the faction which aligned itself with the Holy Roman Emperors. The views here are

The waters of the Tettuccio thermal establishment (these pages) were already famous in the late fourteenth century. Its Art Nouveau murals (opposite) are deliciously wicked; its reading room induces calm, while refreshment awaits in the drinking room and at the fountain.

*T*he much adorned Excelsior establishment (left) *was built in 1909 and enlarged in 1968. The rooms of the Tettuccio* (above) *constantly echo to the waltz music of Johann Strauss.*

particularly magnificent, encompassing Serravalle, Pistoia and Florence to the east and to the west the belfries and towers of Altopascio, Buggiano, Montecarlo, Borgo, Massa Cozzile and Colle.

South-east of Montecatini lies another spa resort of some importance, that of Monsummano Terme which, again, has an old town perched high on a hill. Its fame as a spa is derived from the presence of an underground lake whose waters are reputed to cure both gout and

The old town of Montecatini Alto (right) *clusters around its twelfth-century church of San Niccolò. About four kilometres away is the spa at Monsummano Terme* (below), *named after the local poet Giuseppe Giusto, born there in 1809; its springs are extremely warm and sulphurous.*

Although the main reason for visiting Montecatini is to take the waters (these pages), *neighbouring towns and villages offer other delights, like the church of San Michele at Serravalle* (overleaf).

rheumatism. The principal thermal establishment is named after the local poet, Giuseppe Giusti (1809–50), who is also commemorated in the church of Santa Maria della Fontenuova. Fewer than four kilometres north-east of the new town stands Monsummano Alto on a high hill amid cypresses, junipers and broom, notable for its medieval fortress and the charming twelfth-century Romanesque church. Its position on the western edge of the Montalbino chain yields magnificent views of the lower valley of the Arno and the Valdinievole.

Pescia

LIKE MANY A Tuscan town, medieval Pescia was often a pawn in the struggles for power between Lucca, Pisa and Florence. It was declared a *città* in 1699 and became the seat of a bishop in 1726. Today, it is known as 'the city of flowers', boasting the largest flower market in Italy, famous for its lilies, gladioli and carna-

tions. A tourist resort as well as a horticultural community, it is the principal town of the Valdinievole.

The town is divided in two by the river Pescia. On the left bank rises the architecturally complex cathedral, which began as a Romanesque building but later acquired a Baroque interior in 1693. Its mighty

campanile was added in the eighteenth century on the base of a 1306 construction, and the Renaissance-style façade in the nineteenth. Inside, the Baroque fantasy is especially delightful; the treasures of the interior include the Turini chapel, built by Giuliano di Baccio d'Agnolo in the fifteenth century and now housing the sixteenth-century mausoleum of Baldassare Turini, created by Raffaello da Montelupo. The *Madonna del Baldacchino* is a copy by Pietro Dandini of a painting by Raphael in the Pitti Palace in Florence. The diocesan library and museum are close by, with fifteenth- and sixteenth-century sculptures, as well as paintings from the same era.

Principal town of the Valdinievole region, Pescia is a centre for horticulture and paper-making. The Pescia river divides the town into ecclesiastical and civic centres (overleaf).

The many facets of Pescia: the main town (above *and* overleaf) *lies along the river of the same name. Within are many intriguing lanes and alleys, while fishing is possible in the waters above the town* (right above *and* below).

*P*escia's immediate surroundings include delightful
woods, olive groves, and charming hamlets
like Boveglio, hidden in the mountains north of the
neighbouring village of Collodi (these pages).

Another major church, famous for its paintings of
six scenes from the life of St. Francis, is the Gothic San
Francesco in the Via Battista. Begun in 1211, the church
was not finished until 1632. Bonaventura Berlinghieri
painted the panel of the scenes from the life of the saint
in 1235, a mere nine years after his death; they may
therefore be the most authentic likeness we have. Seek
out the Cappella Cardini, which may have been
designed by Andrea Cavalcanti Buggiano (the adopted
son of Brunelleschi) in 1451. In a chapel of the apse are
fifteenth-century frescoes by Bicci di Lorenzo. Nearby
is the graceful eighteenth-century Teatro Pacini. Well
worth a visit is the little mid-fourteenth-century
church of Sant'Antonio Abate, close to San Francesco,
where fifteenth-century frescoes chronicle the life of

These six scenes from the life of St. Francis of Assisi (above) *in the church of San Francesco were painted by Bonaventura Berlinghieri a mere nine years after the death of the saint. More* treasures of religious art are to be found in the oratory church of Sant' Antonio Abate: *a* Crucifixion *and a* Deposition from the Cross (right above *and* below).

St. Anthony Abbot. Here, too, is a touching thirteenth-century *Deposition from the Cross*, sculpted in wood.

On the right bank of the river is the Piazza Mazzini, enormous, long and narrow, surrounded by buildings dating from the thirteenth to the nineteenth centuries; now the town hall, the Palazzo dei Vicari has a particu-

larly attractive façade, embellished with armorial crests. Here, too, is the oratory of the Madonna di Piè di Piazza, designed in 1447, again by Buggiano. Above the high altar is a fifteenth-century fresco of the *Virgin Mary* which also, delightfully, includes a view of Pescia itself. Close by is the Palazzo Geleotti, the Museo

Civico, in the Piazza Santo Stefano, where medieval and Renaissance works of art are displayed. The *palazzo* also serves as the town library, holding some thirty thousand volumes, including incunabula, miniatures, manuscripts and codices.

Six kilometres west of Pescia is the village of Collodi, also the pen-name of Carlo Lorenzini, creator of Pinocchio, commemorated by the Pinocchio park. And twelve kilometres north of the town is Castelvecchio, notable for its Romanesque church.

The formal and the informal: a wedding couple pose in the Baroque garden of the Villa Garzoni at Collodi (opposite); in a quiet moment the salt and tobacco vendor takes stock of his neighbourhood in Pescia (right). The Garzoni gardens were first laid out in the mid seventeenth century, then reshaped in 1786 by Ottaviano Diodati, with yew trees, hedges, topiary, and superb fountains.

The cathedral of Pontrémoli dominates the town (left *and* below), *its Baroque cupola contrasting strangely with the far older campanile.*

Pontrémoli

SURROUNDED BY THE Apennine mountains and most immediately circled by foothills thick with chestnut trees and by terraced hillsides, Pontrémoli, the main town of the Lunigiana valley, sits at the confluence of the rivers Verde and Magra. It is a place of slate-roofed houses, palaces, towers, attractive streets, some of them arched, and the bridges which cross the two rivers. The town first appears in written history in 990 and passed through turbulent times during the struggles of the Middle Ages. Today, it is a centre of the book trade, offering several annual literary prizes.

The old walls of the town, called 'Cacciaguerra', were built by Castruccio Castracani from Lucca in 1322 to separate the Guelphs in the territory above from the Ghibellines below. Around the centre – the Piazza della Repubblica and the cathedral – are several splendid sixteenth- and seventeenth-century *palazzi*. One of the most remarkable buildings of the town is the Castello del Piagnaro, which dates from the tenth century and today houses a museum of prehistoric statue-menhirs from the surrounding region, some sculpted in human form (notably women and warriors), dating from 1500 B.C. to A.D. 100.

The town's Baroque cathedral received the embellishment of a Neoclassical façade in 1881; its bell-tower was once part of the old fourteenth-century walls. Its bronze door has eight panels depicting the sorrows of the Blessed Virgin Mary. Inside the cathedral is a riot

*T*he Magra (opposite) *is one of two rivers whose confluence is at Pontrémoli, the other being the Verde. Balconied houses* (right) *overlook it near the Ponte del Giubileo; another elegant arch is that of the bridge of San Francesco di Sopra* (below).

W herever one looks in
Pontrémoli, there seem to
be balconies, whether overhanging
the narrow streets (above) or the
rivers which bisect the town (right
and opposite). Another elaborately
appointed balcony and doorway
(above right) fronts the door of the
episcopal palace.

of stucco and marble. Notable are an altar of 1654
in the north transept, and another altarpiece dating
from the seventeenth century in one of the north
chapels. Opposite the cathedral stands the Neoclassical
episcopal palace.

Apart from its cathedral, Pontrémoli is rich indeed
in splendid church architecture. San Francesco has a
Romanesque bell-tower, as well as three aisles in the
contemporary Franciscan fashion. The church was
enlarged in the fifteenth century; its present portico
and façade were added by Giovanni Battista Natali
in 1740. On the second altar on the north side is a
striking fifteenth-century polychrome bas-relief of the

The local life of Pontrémoli is centred on the Piazza della Repubblica (left above *and* below), *a bustling place of newspaper vendors and conversationalists, whose favourite meeting place is the Caffé degli Svizzeri.*

Madonna and Child, probably by Agostino di Duccio. Notable in the apse is a mid-eighteenth-century painting by the Veronese artist Gianbettino Cignaroli of *St. Francis Receiving the Stigmata.*

The Madonna del Ponte (also known as Nostra Donna) is an exquisite oval-shaped Rococo church, dating from 1738 – another design by Giovanni Battista Natali; it contains frescoes by the Florentine Sebastiano Galeotti. Yet another church, Santissima Annunziata (one and a half kilometres south of Pontrémoli) is well worth a visit. Consecrated in 1524, it was built to celebrate a vision of the Blessed Virgin Mary on that very spot. Inside is a tabernacle of 1527 said to be the work of Jacopo Sansovino.

EXORN. MDCCCLXXXI · HONORIFICENTIA POPULI NOSTRI · PERFECT. MCMXXXVI

*P*ontrémoli's cathedral is a mainly Baroque affair,
but its façade (above) is Neoclassical, an 1881
addition by Vicenzo Michele. The two statues flanking
the doorway are by the Seravezza sculptor Antonio Bucci.
Most places in the centre of Pontrémoli yield interesting
details: an elaborate altarpiece in San Geminiano
(right); a plaque to Giuseppe Garibaldi in the entrance
to the Palazzo Comunale (far right). The backdrop to
the town is formed by the Apennines (overleaf), notably
Monte Orsaro and Monte Marmagna.

San Casciano

IN VAL DI PESA

SET HIGH ON ITS EMINENCE between the valleys of the Greve and the Pesa, the entrancing town of San Casciano overlooks the hills of Chianti. From the terrace of its Piazza della Repubblica a view of the valley of the Pesa delightfully unfolds itself. Once a country seat of the bishops of Florence, San Casciano came under the suzerainty of that city in 1272. Its fortifications, begun in 1343, were subsequently enlarged and much strengthened over the centuries, especially by Cosimo I in the sixteenth; their walls still stand, incorporating one of the original defensive gateways to the town.

*T*he surroundings of San Casciano are certainly as interesting as the town itself; there can be few finer sights in the whole of Tuscany than the abbey of San Michele at Passignano, caught in the evening light (opposite). The abbey was originally founded in 1049 by St. Giovanni Gualberto of the Vallombrosan order, rebuilt in the thirteenth century and added to in the nineteenth. Another fine building close to San Casciano is the Castello di Bibbione (right). The town itself is full of lanes and alleys, like the Via Lucardesi (below).

VERGINE IMMACOLATA

*T*he Chiesino (opposite) *in the Piazza dell' Erbe is part of the old town walls. In the midst of the town's antiquity, though, the present day goes about its business: the market in the Piazza della Repubblica* (above); *children play in the abbey grounds at Passignano* (right).

The centre of the town is mainly notable for its splendid churches, although more secular pleasures also abound, such as the animated market on the Piazza della Repubblica, where stalls offer virtually everything you ever need to buy, from clothes to local produce. It is the churches, however, that dominate the old centre. There is San Francesco and its campanile, raised in 1492. The church of Santa Maria del Gesù in the Via Roma now serves as a museum of religious art, housing masterpieces drawn from neighbouring churches, including a *Coronation of the Virgin Mary* by Neri di Bicci from the late fifteenth century. Reached from the Piazza Orazio Perozzi is Santa Maria del Prato (known locally as the Misericordia), built in the fourteenth-century Tuscan-Gothic style and rebuilt in the sixteenth century. Again, it houses some

*T*hese scenes convey some of the delights of the countryside surrounding San Casciano: a rural shrine at Bargino (left); the road to Mercantale (below); olive groves at Peppoli Antinori (right).

fine religious art, notably a *Crucifixion* of 1325 by Simone Martini.

It is in its surroundings that the full charm of San Casciano is realized. From the town a number of attractive by-roads lead to exquisite dependent villages and hamlets. To the north, for instance, is the Romanesque church of Santa Maria at Decimo (see pp.2-3) with its associated farm buildings. The gem of the region, however, must surely be the Vallombrosan monastery and abbey church of San Michele at Passignano. The complex of buildings stands amid slopes of vineyards and clusters of cypresses; in spite of its apparently ancient aspect, substantial parts of what we see today were added in the late nineteenth century, when the monastery was a private residence. Originally Romanesque, the church itself was much modified in the sixteenth century. But whatever the architectural origins of this delightful place, the sight of the abbey at Passignano caught in the rays of the evening sun must stand as one of the most memorable in the whole of Tuscany.

San Miniato

ONCE KNOWN AS San Miniato al Tedesco ('of the German'), when the town was one of the residences of the German Holy Roman Emperors, impressive San Miniato stands high on a hill overlooking the Arno valley. This remarkably attractive town grew up around an eighth-century church over the shrine of a martyr. From its hill are magical views of the sea, the hills of Fiesole, Volterra and the Apuan Alps. Dominating the valley, the town is itself dominated by the remains of the thirteenth-century castle built for the Emperor Frederick II. Dante tells the story in his *Inferno* of Pier delle Vigne, Frederick's chancellor, who was falsely accused of treason, blinded on the orders of

the Emperor, and then committed suicide in the taller of the two remaining fortified towers.

The larger tower, a post-World War II reconstruction, is circled by gardens. The smaller, the Torre di Matilde, is now the campanile of the cathedral. As the name of the tower indicates, San Miniato was the birthplace in 1046 of Countess Matilda, whose piety led her to give a substantial portion of her wealth to Pope Gregory VII. Begun as a Romanesque building in the twelfth century, the cathedral now has a mid-nineteenth-century neo-Baroque interior, though it retains its brick Romanesque façade, embellished with majolica and marble statues. Its door-ways were rebuilt

Deriving its name from the Christian martyr St. Minias, San Miniato occupies a typically strategic position on a hill (opposite). Especially prominent in the town is the church of San Francesco (above); dating originally from the late thirteenth century, it displays all the stern austerity of Franciscan architecture.

*V*iewed from the Rocca, the Santuario del Crocifisso stands close to the Torre di Matilde, now the cathedral's campanile (right). *Ecclesiastical San Miniato: classical* doorways embellish the brick façade of the essentially Romanesque cathedral (above); a priest walks home (for lunch?) outside fourteenth-century San Domenico (below).

in the fifteenth century; inside are fine sixteenth-century paintings. Beside the cathedral stands the twelfth-century episcopal palace. On the other side is the diocesan museum, whose collection is composed of masterpieces from local churches. Its treasures include works by Fra Bartolomeo, Neri di Bicci and Filippo Lippi. Close by is the twelfth-century Palazzo dei Vicari dell'Imperatore, once the home of

the Emperor's representatives, the Imperial Vicars. The Piazza della Repubblica is flanked by the Palazzo del Seminario which rises above the façades of medieval shops.

San Miniato is especially rich in fine churches and they constitute the main reason for lingering here. San Domenico is the church of the Piazza del Popolo, reached from the Piazza della Repubblica by the Via

*T*he painted façade of the seventeenth-century
Seminario (above left *and* top) *rises above
fourteenth-century shops. And amid all the fine buildings
there is still time for a game of football* (above).

The Baroque forms of the Santuario del Crocifisso contrast with the starker presence of the Torre di Matilde (right). In the former's interior the cupola is embellished by an eighteenth-century fresco of the Ascension by Antonio Domenico Bamberini (opposite). Other treasures of the town include fourteenth-century frescoes in the council chamber of the Palazzo Comunale (below right), and this thirteenth-century painting of St. Michael the Archangel Slaying the Devil by Bartolomeo Sprengher (below) in the church of San Francesco.

Conti. Begun in the late twelfth century, its façade still awaits its cladding. Inside is the fifteenth-century tomb of Giovanni Chellini, perhaps (very intriguing) designed by Donatello, for it is the body of his Florentine doctor which lies in the tomb. The frescoes date from the seventeenth and eighteenth centuries. Another frescoed building is the charming Lorentino church, built in the fourteenth century. The Santuario del Crocifisso, the seventeenth-century crucifix chapel, can be reached by steps to the left of the cathedral. Built by Antonio Maria Ferri between 1705 and 1718, the sanctuary houses one of the town's most important relics, a crucifix thought to have helped the community to escape the worst ravages of the plague of 1637. The Romanesque-Gothic San Francesco is also well worth a visit. On a slightly more secular note, the Palazzo Comunale should not be missed, if only because of the frescoes in the council chamber.

Sansepolcro

The municipal authority of Sansepolcro is housed in the magnificently porticoed Mannerist Palazzo delli Laudi (left), *begun by Alberto Alberti in 1592 and completed by Antonio Cantagallina in 1609. The loggia* (below) *is especially elegant. Next door is the cathedral, with its rose-window.*

SITUATED ON THE BORDER OF Tuscany and Umbria, on the banks of the upper valley of the Tiber, this charming fifteenth-century town is famous for its fabulous artistic treasures. It was the birthplace and, for a time, home of Piero della Francesca, one of the greatest painters of the Quattrocento, who died there in 1492. He lies buried in the Capella di San Leonardo, named after the saint who by tradition cared for the Holy Sepulchre in Jerusalem. Indeed, Sansepolcro ('Holy Sepulchre') derives its name from relics brought

The vignettes of Sansepolcro are plentiful and characterful: walking the dog in the Piazza del Ponte (above); merchandise in the Via XX Settembre (above right); Amleto delle Piano, stonemason, in the Via Giuseppe Mazzini (centre right); the workshop of Paolo Giovagnini (right); the flying arches which span the Via del Buon Umore (opposite).

from what was allegedly the tomb of Jesus in Jerusalem in the tenth century by two pilgrims.

Though badly damaged by earthquakes in the fourteenth century, as well as suffering bomb damage in World War II, the town still has many fine old houses, *palazzi* and a sixteenth-century Medici fortress (possibly designed by Giuliano da Sangallo). The Via XX Settembre, which stretches from the Porta Fiorentina to the Porta Romana, is lined with many of the town's finest Gothic and Renaissance buildings. The narrow Via del Buon Umore runs beneath delightful brick

The main altar of the cathedral (opposite) is a magnificent Baroque creation; another treasure there is the wooden Volto Santo *(above).* But the greatest treasure of all is certainly Piero della Francesca's *Resurrection (above) in the Museo Civico. And outside the town are splendid sights of a different nature (overleaf).*

arches. The Mannerist Palazzo delle Laudi has an arcaded courtyard. Its immediate neighbour, the town's eleventh-century cathedral of St. John the Baptist, remarkable for a brilliant rose-window, is a mixture of Romanesque and Gothic, though much changed over the centuries. It began life as a Camaldolese abbey, whose monks cared for the Jerusalem relics. There are a tabernacle and statues of St. Romuald and St. Benedict from the della Robbia workshop in the cathedral, as well as an *Ascension* thought to be by Perugino. Among the many other works of religious art housed there is a great wooden crucifix, the *Volto Santo*, dating, at least in part, from the tenth century. These are also fourteenth- and fifteenth-century frescoes, including a *Crucifixion* by Bartolomeo della Gatta.

The splendours of the cathedral interior are reflected in the treasures of other churches in Sansepolcro. San Lorenzo has a sixteenth-century *Deposition from the Cross* by Rosso Fiorentino; San Francesco is renowned for its thirteenth-century façade and campanile. And close by is Santa Maria delle Grazie, with a charming double loggia and a superb high altar by a local artist, Raffaellino del Colle. The sixteenth-century wooden ceiling is by Alberto Alberti.

The finest works of art in Sansepolcro, however, are the paintings by Piero della Francesca in the Museo Civico, especially his *Resurrection*. But Piero's pre-eminence should not detract from the works of other remarkable locally born artists, whose masterpieces are also displayed in the museum. Among these works are paintings by Signorelli, Matteo di Giovanni and Pontormo.

CENTRAL TUSCANY

The turbulence and warfare of past times seriously affected the development of the towns of central Tuscany, as Etruscan fought Roman, as the fifth-century Barbarian invasions swept southwards, as Florentine fought Sienese, and – as if the foregoing were not enough – the Germans and the Allies passed through in the mid twentieth century. Many of these towns are sited defensively on hills; certainly the most significant have been fortified at one time or another. Both Etruscan and medieval walls surround parts of Volterra; the thirteenth-century walls of Monteriggioni, which still encircle the town, so impressed contemporaries that Dante mentioned them in his Divine Comedy; Castiglion Fiorentino was first fortified against the Barbarians, and then received a citadel in the Middle Ages; Certaldo suffered damage during World War II, but the walls of the old town remain remarkably intact; and the massive gateway of the Porta Nuova still stands in the upper town of Colle di Val d'Elsa.

Distinguished religious architecture, Romanesque and Gothic, sits cheek by jowl with monuments to secular power. The palazzi of Montepulciano and Volterra may impress by their profusion, but the Palazzo Comunale at Castiglion Fiorentino and the Palazzo Pretorio of Certaldo are especially imposing. In the same towns are the Romanesque and Gothic splendours of, respectively, the San Francesco and the Santi Tommaso e Prospero churches. And, remember, these fascinating towns are set in a richly endowed landscape of olive groves, vineyards and orchards.

The undulating strada panoramica *sweeps round the west side of Certaldo* (opposite).

Castiglion Fiorentino

*O**ne of the town's most advantageous viewing places is the elegant sixteenth-century Logge del Vasari (left and below). Among the various views it discloses are those of the collegiate church of San Giuliano, with a campanile only completed in 1930, and of the valley of the Chio.*

THE CHARMS OF Castiglion Fiorentino are not confined to the streets within its medieval battlemented walls; all around spread the splendid slopes of the Valdichiana, planted with pines, olives and vines. Mention of this attractive market town first appears in 1014; later it was to become yet another acquisition of Florence, in 1384. Signs of a turbulent though undoubtedly rich history are everywhere: a considerable stretch of the old walls still stands, as does a single tower of the old citadel, built in the eleventh and twelfth centuries. More tranquil times are reflected in the architecture of the principal square, the Piazza del

*T*he octagonal church of the
Madonna della Consolazione
(above left), *attributed to Antonio
da Sangallo the Younger, stands
near the Porta Romana.*

*T*he olive harvest around *Castiglion Fiorentino* (opposite left *and* above); *in the background to these olive groves looms the castle of Montecchio Vesponi, given in gratitude by the Florentines to Sir John Hawkwood, the English mercenary, in 1375.*

Municipio, in which we find the impressive sixteenth-century Palazzo Comunale and the graceful Logge del Vasari, decorated with coats of arms and a fresco of the *Annunciation*. It discloses a fine view of the valley of the Chio.

The churches of Castiglion Fiorentino are justly famous for the wealth of art treasures they contain. Foremost among them is the collegiate church of San

Giuliano, restored in a classical style in 1853, which holds paintings by Lorenzo di Credi (notably, *Mary and Joseph Adoring the Infant Jesus*), by Bartolomeo della Gatta and by Segna di Bonaventura. Beside the collegiate church are the remains of the Pieve, which contains a fresco of the *Deposition from the Cross* by the school of Luca Signorelli. Another delightful church is the part Romanesque, part Gothic San Francesco;

*S*unrise over Castiglion Fiorentino reveals a town dominated by the towers of the collegiate church to the left and the eleventh- and twelfth-century Torre del Cassero to the right (preceding pages).

scenes from the saint's life abound there: twenty-six frescoes in the cloisters, and a likeness by Margaritone d'Arezzo, dating from the 1280s. Near the Porta Romana stands the octagonal church of the Madonna della Consolazione, possibly based on a design by Antonio da Sangallo the Younger.

More examples of the fabulous art patrimony of the town are to be found in the Pinacoteca Comunale,

*T*he architectural austerity of the Franciscans informs the church of San Francesco (above). Basically Romanesque, it also incorporates some Gothic elements of the second half of the thirteenth century. In the Via San Michele (right): a bakery proclaims its use of a wood oven; a cat enjoys the afternoon sun. The Via del Cassero (opposite), with drinking fountain, leads up to the Chiesa di Sant' Angelo. Note how ingeniously the irregular, rough-hewn stones are set together.

The artistic patrimony of Castiglion Fiorentino is fabulous: a fifteenth-century Madonna and Child with Saints *by the studio of Matteo di Giovanni in the Pinacoteca Comunale* (left); *also in the Pinacoteca is* St. Francis Receiving the Stigmata *by Bartolomeo della Gatta, 1486* (detail, opposite).

Another painting by della Gatta in the Pinacoteca is the c. 1480 St. Michael the Archangel *(detail, above).* Yet another della Gatta is in the collegiate church of San Giuliano: his Virgin with Son Enthroned, with SS. Peter, Paul, Julian and Michael *(detail, left).*

entered by way of the church of Sant'Angelo. Here is a magnificent seventeenth-century high altar by Filippo Berrettini and a thirteenth-century painted cross. The pre-eminent biographer of the Italian Renaissance, Vasari, is represented by a *Madonna and Child* (guarded by Saints Anthony and Silvester). More treasures await in the Pinacoteca itself, including paintings by Bartolomeo della Gatta and Giovanni di Paolo.

About four kilometres to the south of the town lies the castle of Montecchio Vesponi, given by the grateful people of Florence to the famous English mercenary, Sir John Hawkwood, in 1375. Hawkwood died in 1394 and was eventually buried in England, but later commemorated in the Duomo of Florence by an equestrian statue.

Certaldo

Whether visiting the lower or the upper part of this striking brick-built town set amid the olive groves and cypresses of the Elsa valley, it is impossible to escape the references to the local celebrity – Boccaccio. Born in Paris, the author of the *Decameron* eventually retired to the narrow, winding streets of this delightful hill-town, where he died on 21 December 1375. In the lower town, prosperous and industrial, he is commemorated by a late nineteenth-century marble statue in the Piazza Boccaccio. In the upper is the Casa-museo di Boccaccio which recreates the circumstances of his life and serves as the national centre for Boccaccio studies, with a library and displays of illustrations by various hands of his work.

S et amid cypress and olive groves (below and right), Certaldo makes a beguiling sight on its hill at sunset.

The presence of Boccaccio is everywhere in Certaldo; this portrait bust (left) in the church of Santi Michele e Jacopo was sculpted by Giovanni Francesco Rustici in 1503, 128 years after its subject's death.

He lies buried in the nearby thirteenth-century church of Santi Michele e Jacopo. Boccaccio's tomb was desecrated in 1783 by people scandalized by his writings, so the present slab is modern; a portrait bust of the author by Giovanni Francesco Rustici dates from 1503. The church has a number of other treasures: a fourteenth-century Sienese fresco of the *Madonna and Child*, and two tabernacles and an altarpiece from the workshop of the della Robbia family. There is also an interesting urn which houses the corpse of the Blessed Giulia. She lived for thirty years walled up in a cell in prayer; when she died in 1367, it is said that every church bell in Certaldo miraculously rang.

Ancient brickwork proliferates in this town – here on the west side (below). Brick, too, is the façade of the Palazzo Pretorio (opposite), rising above its early-fifteenth-century loggia. The escutcheons mounted on the brickwork, in glazed terracotta or stone, display the arms of the Florentine governors of the town.

COMUNE DI CERTALDO
ASSESSORATO ALLA CULTURA
PALAZZO PRETORIO

ESPONE

GIOBBI
USA
10-06-9-07

Certaldo's Palazzo Pretorio was rebuilt in the fifteenth century, its courtyard decorated in that era with frescoes by Pier Francesco Fiorentino. Spirited coats of arms (some in terracotta, some in stone) adorn its battlemented façade and its courtyard, most of them of the Florentine notables who governed the town. The tower of the *palazzo* offers superb views of the town and the river valley. In the rooms surrounding the courtyard and in the neighbouring chapel are the remains of paintings by Benozzo Gozzoli and Giusto d'Andrea. Here, too, are cells in which prisoners carved messages on the walls, and splendid doorways and fireplaces.

*M*ore coats of arms embellish the loggia of the Palazzo Pretorio (opposite) *and the well-worn entrance to its chapel* (right). *More intimate notes are struck by the presence of the custodian's somnolent cat* (above) *and the dilapidation of this fountain in the garden of the Palazzo Stiozzi Ridolfi* (below).

The main street of the upper town (these pages) *is named, inevitably, Via Boccaccio, after Certaldo's most famous son. As we look down the street* (opposite), *the writer's former house is surmounted by the second tower on the right*

In all, this country town is an exquisite survival of the Middle Ages, somehow haunted by the spirit of a man who seems at all times to have been an unassuming genius. It is entirely appropriate that the main street of the upper town, lined with some fine houses, should be known as the Via Boccaccio. And there is no better way to savour the unique *frisson* which Certaldo yields than to view the landscape from the Val d'Elsa to San Gimignano from the garden of the Palazzo Pretorio and, then, to enter the delicious thirteenth-century church of Santi Tommaso e Prospero to view the remains of the Gozzoli frescoes.

Colle di Val d'Elsa

COLLE IS VERY MUCH A TOWN of two contrasting parts: upper and lower. The latter is chiefly modern, renowned now for its glassware, which has been produced in the town since the fourteenth century. It lies along the valley floor of the river Elsa, the waters of which were canalized in the Middle Ages to serve burgeoning wood and paper trades. Most visitors, however, will concern themselves with the upper town, a captivating gem of a place, built high on a rocky ridge, still retaining its original medieval street plan and a number of fine *palazzi*. Like many a Tuscan town, it was heavily fought over in the late Middle Ages, as its defensive walls testify; it finally fell to the Florentines in 1269 at the Battle of Colle, a bloody revenge for their defeat by the Sienese at Montaperti nine years earlier.

Apart from the animated Piazza Arnolfo di Cambio, named after the town's famous architect son, there is one substantial reason for lingering in the lower town before attempting the ascent to the upper: the thirteenth-century church of Sant'Agostino on the Via dei Fossi, later rebuilt (in 1521) by Antonio da Sangallo the Elder. The original façade remains unfinished, but

Of the town's original ramparts, the castellated Porta Nuova remains impressive (above). *Views of the north side of Colle* (right *and* opposite) *reveal its strategic siting. More intimate is a market stall* (below) *set out in the Piazza Arnolfo di Cambio, named after the town's most famous architect son.*

*These two Madonnas grace, respectively, the upper
and lower towns: the* Madonna del Latte *in
the Via del Castello (above); the* Madonna and Child
*by Taddeo di Bartolo in Sant' Agostino (left). The
unfinished Palazzo Campana (right) by Giuliano di
Baccio d' Agnolo is a Mannerist masterpiece.*

the interior is a marvellous exercise in Renaissance
harmony, punctuated by at least two masterpieces:
an altar with a *Madonna and Child with Saints*
by Taddeo di Bartolo, and a *Deposition with Saints* by
Ridolfo Ghirlandaio. A campanile was added much
later, in 1900.

In contrast, the upper town is so full of treasures
that few people would begrudge the relatively steep
climb needed to reach it. The approach by car or bus
goes by way of the magnificent fortified gateway, the

Porta Nuova, often attributed to Giuliano da Sangallo. The main streets of the town, the Via Gracco del Sacco and the Via del Castello, reveal a series of magnificent town houses. In the tower-house which is no. 63 Via del Castello was born Arnolfo di Cambio, the original architect of the plans for the Florence Duomo in the late thirteenth century and, probably, a substantial influence on the designs of the church of Santa Croce and the Palazzo Vecchio in the same city. The Via Campana leads to a fine bridge which links the eastern and western parts of the town; at its far end stands a Mannerist masterpiece, the Palazzo Campana of 1539, the work of Giuliano di Baccio d'Agnolo.

On the Via del Castello lies the exquisite Romanesque church of Santa Maria in Canonica, notable outside for a fine rose-window set in the stone façade, and inside for a magnificent fifteenth-century tabernacle of the *Madonna and Child with Saints* by Pier Francesco Fiorentino. The street eventually opens out into the Piazza del Duomo and its collection of important buildings.

*T*he Romanesque church of Santa Maria in Canonica stands on a corner of the Piazza di Canonica (opposite), *its façade decorated with brick and blind arches. Inside is a fifteenth-century altar painting,* Madonna and Child with Saints, *by Pier Francesco Fiorentino (above).*

A steep climb via the lane known as the Costa (below) *connects the lower and upper towns.*

The Duomo itself was originally a Romanesque structure; traces of its origins can still be seen in the arcades on the northern side. In the early seventeenth century, however, it was effectively transformed into an elegant example of Baroque, filled with a number of outstanding art treasures. There is a bronze lectern by Pietro Tacca, a pupil of Giambologna, who was probably responsible for the design of the bronze *Crucifix* over the high altar, perhaps the chief glory of the cathedral. A marble pulpit of 1465, standing on pillars and capitals from an earlier structure, has fine bas-reliefs, probably by the Florentine master Giuliano da Maiano. In the south transept is the tabernacle of the Santo Chiodo (Holy Nail), designed by Mino da Fiesole to hold a fragment of one of the nails which held Jesus on the Cross. The campanile dates from the seventeenth century.

A basket-maker of the new town: Ezio Batoni surveys the world as it passes by his premises in the Via Rosselli (above).

*B*oreno Cigni practices the craft *of glass-engraving in the Vicolo delle Fontanelle* (below).

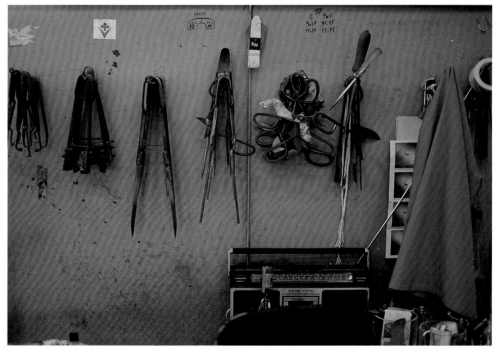

Close to the cathedral stands the fourteenth-century Palazzo Pretorio, now the town's archaeological museum. The civic museum and sacred art gallery are housed in the Palazzo dei Priori. And there are more art treasures in the form of frescoes by Bartolo di Fredi in the Palazzo Vescovile (the former episcopal palace).

As an end-note to Colle di Val d'Elsa, there can be none more exquisite than a visit to the church and monastery of San Francesco. Reached via an old stone bridge, the church itself has a Romanesque sandstone façade and Renaissance cloisters. Inside, the great treasure is undoubtedly the altarpiece of the *Madonna and Child with Four Saints* of 1479 by Sano di Pietro. Even if there were no other art and architectural treasures in Colle di Val d'Elsa, the sight of this illumination of the lives of the saints would always make a visit well worthwhile.

*A*t Gracciano, craftsmen *continue the local traditions of glass-making at the Vilca works* (top *and* above).

Montepulciano

Viewed from this angle (left), Montepulciano appears dominated by the fourteenth-century campanile of its cathedral. Entrance to the town is most picturesquely achieved by way of the Porta al Prato (below), the work of Antonio da Sangallo the Elder and part of the ramparts designed by the same architect.

ONE OF TUSCANY's most attractive towns, Montepulciano dominates the pass between the Val d'Asso and the Val di Chiana. Henry James described it as 'brown and queer and crooked, and noble withal.' Small wonder that Siena and Florence competed to own the town, until Florence finally prevailed in 1511. Set on a tufa escarpment garlanded by cypress trees, protected by walls and gates, Montepulciano is arranged along a main street, with side-streets and alleys which lead to the walls. It is now the centre of thriving vineyards, producing the celebrated Vino Nobile and the Brunello. At no. 1 Via Poliziano, was born the most famous son of Montepulciano, Angelo Ambrogini, poet and friend of Botticelli, who assumed the name 'Poliziano'. He saved the life of Lorenzo the Magnificent when enemies murdered the latter's brother in Florence cathedral.

Entrance to the northern, lower end of the town is gained via the Porta al Prato, designed by Antonio da Sangallo the Elder. Just to the north stands the fourteenth-century church of Sant'Agnese, with cloisters and seventeenth-century frescoes depicting the life of the town's patron saint, St. Agnese (1268–1317) who is buried in the church. She was canonized in 1726. Once inside the gateway, the main street (known as the Corso) rises past superb *palazzi*, the architectural legacy of the Florentine influence. Another reminder of Florence is the Colonna del Marzocco, which bears the heraldic lion (*marzocco*) of that city.

When the Florentine Antonio da Sangallo the Elder took up residence in Montepulciano in 1511 with a

M *ontepulciano commands views over rolling countryside, sometimes punctuated by intriguing detail, especially during the olive harvest (these pages).*

A terracotta relief of Madonna and Child with Saints Augustine and John the Baptist by Michelozzo di Bartolomeo crowns the doorway of Sant' Agostino (right). Travestine stone is the material of the entrance to Santa Lucia (below), designed by Flaminio del Turco in 1653. The tower of the Palazzo Comunale (opposite) offers views as far as Siena, sixty-five kilometres north-east.

commission to rebuild the town gates and walls, he was also engaged by the local notables to work on their *palazzi*. In the northern part of the town he designed the Palazzo Cocconi; further south, on the Via di Volaia section of the Corso, is his Palazzo Cervini, built for Cardinal Marcello Cervini, who became Pope Marcello Cervini, unusually retaining his baptismal name. He died a mere twenty-two days after his election. Another Sangallo *palazzo* is the Contucci, on the Piazza Grande, designed for Cardinal Maria Giovanni del Monte, later Pope Julius III, notorious for his infatuation with a fifteen-year-old Parma street urchin. Jacopo Vignola also contributed to the town's architectural patrimony: the Palazzo Tarugi in the Piazza Grande (though some attribute this to Sangallo the Elder), and the Palazzo Avignonesi, at the northern end of the Corso.

To the west of the Corso, on the Piazza Michelozzo, lies the church of Sant'Agostino. Its façade and the terracotta relief over the door, depicting the *Madonna and Child with Saints Augustine and John the Baptist*, are by Michelozzo di Bartolomeo. There is a crucifix on the high altar, attributed to Sangallo the Elder; other notable works include a *Crucifixion* by Lorenzo di Credi and a *St. Bernardino* by Giovanni di Paolo. Across the *piazza*, above the medieval Torre di Pulcinella, an effigy of the *commedia dell'arte* clown strikes the town bell on the hour.

Montepulciano's main square, the Piazza Grande, is a vibrant place offering a diversity of pleasures, from wine-tasting in the Palazzo Contucci, savouring the art treasures of the Duomo, to viewing the surrounding countryside from the tower of the Palazzo Comunale. The cathedral, its façade still unfinished, was built between 1592 and 1630 to the plans of Ippolito Scalza. Its finest treasure is undoubtedly the triptych behind the high altar by the Sienese Taddeo di Bartolo showing the *Assumption of the Virgin with Saints*. Other

masterpieces (by, among others, Benedetto da Maiano and Sano di Pietro), in particular a superb *Madonna del Pilastro,* can be found in various parts of the interior. Opposite the Palazzo Contucci on the Piazza Grande rises the powerful three-storeyed Palazzo Comunale, begun in the fourteenth century and finished by Michelozzo in 1425 with embellishments which recall the Palazzo Vecchio in Florence. Its square tower offers splendid views of Lake Trasimeno, Siena and Cortona. Another famous sight of the main square is the lion-and-griffin well next to the Palazzo Tarugi. As well as the lions of Florence and the griffins of Montepulciano,

note too the heraldic shield with the six balls of the Medici. Just before the Piazza Grande, in the Via Ricci, the Museo Civico is housed in the fourteenth-century brick and travertine Palazzo Neri-Orselli. Perhaps the finest masterpiece on display is a *Madonna and Child with Angels* by the school of Duccio.

A short walk to the west of the town lies one of the great architectural treasures of the Renaissance in Italy: the church of San Biagio, a supreme design achievement and a marvellous sight to end any visit to Montepulciano. Commissioned in 1518 by the Ricci nobles of the town, the church was the major project of

*M*ontepulciano is rich indeed in church architecture. To the north of the Porta al Prato is fourteenth-century Sant' Agnese, named after the patron saint of the town, who originally founded a Dominican convent on the site. The cloister (left) is decorated with seventeenth-century frescoes. The town's real jewel, though, is the church of San Biagio, one of the great treasures of the Italian Renaissance. Designed by Antonio da Sangallo the Elder, its tower (opposite) incorporates several orders of arcihtecture: Doric, Ionic, Corinthian and Composite.

architect Antonio da Sangallo until his death in 1534. The main plan of the church is that of a Greek cross, topped by a central dome; the main façade and sides are beautifully articulated in honey-coloured stone. Inside, the harmonious lines of the exterior are contin-

ued around the centrepiece of the marble high altar created in 1584 by Gianozzo and Lisandro di Pietra Albertini; a final flourish is the fourteenth-century fresco in the tabernacle of the *Madonna and Child with St. Francis*.

The centrepiece of the interior of San Biagio is the marble high altar (left), designed in 1584 by Gianozzo and Lisandro di Pietra Albertini. Later, in 1617, statues of SS. John the Baptist, Agnes, Catherine of Siena, and George by Ottaviano Lazzari were added. The honey-coloured stone of the church make it a striking sight as it sits in countryside just below Montepulciano (opposite). Patterned on a Greek cross, the main church was built between 1518 and 1534. The lantern of the dome and the tower, planned to be one of two, were completed only in 1545 by Baccio d'Agnolo.

Monteriggioni

Dawn comes to Monteriggioni: a hunter stalks his prey (below); the defensive walls and towers – Dante's 'horrible giants' – loom on the skyline to create the impression of a true citadel (opposite).

IN THEIR STRUGGLES with the Florentines during the Middle Ages it is clear that the notables of Siena did not regard the immediate fortifications of their own city as being sufficiently proof against the hostile attentions of the enemy from the north. Reacting to the perceived threat, the Sienese set about ringing themselves with a number of fortified towns which would act both as a deterrent and an early-warning system. The marvellously preserved walled town of

Monteriggioni played a crucial role in this aspect of Siena's strategic planning.

Picturesquely perched amid olive groves, this hill-town made an ideal spot for fortification. The first walls were put in place in the early part of the thirteenth century, but the major part of the construction – huge walls and fourteen towers – was added after the unexpected and bloody defeat of the Florentines by the Sienese at Montaperti in 1260.

A town of few significant streets, Monteriggioni nevertheless yields some picturesque corners, like the Via Matteotti (opposite) and the Largo di Fontebranda (right and right above). Outside the town lies Abbadia a Isola (above), with a gem of a Romanesque church.

The magnitude of the new defences made an immediate impression on the medieval imagination and they promptly made an appearance in Dante's *Inferno*, the towers being likened to 'horrible giants'. Now, vines and trees reach up to the walls, so that the town really does appear from afar like an isolated citadel.

Within the town the streets are cobbled and narrow; gardens lie immediately beneath the walls. In many ways the interior of the town is an unremarkable place: no great palaces, a relatively short main street, an attractive Romanesque parish church, a small public garden. Most important here are the views – both of the town from the surrounding countryside and from the walls over the hill country which is quintessentially Tuscan.

Just to the north of Monteriggioni, in the direction of Poggibonsi, lies the small town of Staggia. Here, the fortifications are Florentine, and several towers and the Rocca of 1432 still survive as ruins.

Elsewhere, the Romanesque church of Santa Maria Assunta and its associated museum contain a number of important art treasures. These include a *St. Mary Magdalene* altarpiece by Antonio del Pollaiuolo and a fourteenth-century Sienese *Madonna and Child*.

In 1705 the English essayist, Joseph Addison, made a very perceptive comment about the Italian landscape: 'One seldom finds in Italy a spot of ground more agreeable than ordinary, that is not covered with a convent.' And, indeed, one very agreeable excursion west from Monteriggioni is to Abbadia a Isola, as the Cistercian abbey of San Salvatore is known, because of its location on an island in the middle of marshland. There is a small village here, but the true gem of the place is the

*T*uscan charm exudes from these details of courtyards at Castiglion Ghinibaldi, near Monteriggioni (this page).

triple-naved church which, though begun in the eleventh century, is largely a creation of rebuilding in the eighteenth. It does, however, contain a superb fresco of the *Madonna and Child* by Taddeo di Bartolo and an early-fifteenth-century baptismal font. In all, it is an entirely satisfactory postscript to an exploration of Monteriggioni and its immediate surroundings.

*M*onteriggioni lies in the midst of vigorously worked agricultural land (these pages). *Even outside the town, the visitor will find many an interesting detail to reflect upon.*

Volterra

WEST OF SIENA LIES THE strange and exciting town of Volterra, famous for its alabaster and a lesson in itself on Tuscan history. All the region's past is here: the Etruscans, the Romans, the Florentines and the glories of the Renaissance. Yet, in spite of its long and complex history, there is an air of impermanence about the place, mainly because of its site; it stands on a bizarre, crumbling ridge (the *Balze*) which in the past caused part of the original town to fall away. Substantial lengths of the Etruscan walls still remain, however, and one of the main gates, the Porta all'Arco, incorporates three Etruscan sculpted heads in its essentially Roman structure. More Roman remains, including those of an amphitheatre, lie to the north of the town walls. And of all the museums of the artefacts of Tuscany's past, the Museo Guarnacci must not be missed; its major

*V*olterra *writ large and in detail: rooftops from the Palazzo dei Priori* (right) *hide the more intimate detailing of the town – here, the well-worn steps near the Fonti San Felice* (below).

collection, bequeathed by a local collector to the town in 1761, is of around 650 Etruscan funerary urns, many of them with sculpted lids of effigies of the dead and friezes of Etruscan life and mythology. The most celebrated exhibit is a terracotta tomb panel depicting a couple, supposedly husband and wife, stoically contemplating death.

In medieval times Volterra prospered, rivalling Florence in prestige and power, though it was overcome by the Florentines in 1361 and again in 1472 by Lorenzo the Magnificent. His legacy to the town is the Rocca Nuova, the fortress he added to the fourteenth-century structure, the Rocca Vecchio, which dominates the south-eastern corner of the town.

*T*he Porta all' Arco (opposite) *is said to be the oldest surviving arch in Italy incorporating substantial Etruscan elements, including the three sculpted heads in its upper part, which was added by the Romans. In this workshop near the arch* (left), *Piero Giani is working in alabaster, continuing an unbroken tradition in the town from pre-Christian times. The colour of the material may vary from ivory-white to pale lemon, orange, green, red and grey-black. The famous Etruscan museum at Volterra lodges a fascinating collection of alabaster funerary urns* (below left *and* right).

*A*round Volterra lie the *crumbling crags* (Balze) (opposite) *which once caused part of the ancient town to collapse. The town's majestic Rocca* (above), *built for Lorenzo the Magnificent in 1472, still looks solid enough; its massive, battlemented tower is known as 'Il Maschio'. The presence of another occupying power in the town is still splendidly evident in the ruins of the former Roman amphitheatre* (right).

Volterra is a treasure-house of medieval and Renaissance religious art. The Duomo alone contains a wealth of masterpieces, including the 1592 ceiling in the Holy Sacrament chapel (opposite), *with stucco-work by Lionello Ricciarelli and frescoes by Giovanni Balducci. There is also a magnificent* Deposition from the Cross (below), *the work of a Pisan sculptor in 1228. In the Palazzo dei Priori the far end of the council chamber* (right) *is decorated with an* Annunciation *by Jacopo di Cione of 1383.*

The church of San Francesco incorporates the chapel of Santa Croce, dating from 1315 and afterwards decorated with frescoes of The Legend of the True Cross (right) *by Cenni di Francesco nearly a century later.*

In the centre of Volterra the hub of life and activity is undoubtedly the exquisite medieval Piazza dei Priori. Here stands the magnificent biscuit-coloured Palazzo dei Priori begun in 1208 and the oldest civic building in Tuscany. Surmounted by a graceful crenellated tower, its façade is decorated with the terracotta and stone coats of arms of the Florentine notables who came to govern the town. Inside, especially in the Sala del Consiglio Comunale (the council chamber), are Florentine and Sienese paintings and frescoes, notably a fine *Annunciation* of 1383 by Jacopo di Cione. Another extraordinary medieval edifice is the thirteenth-century Palazzo Pretorio. Its tower is known as Il Torre Porcellino because of a curious figure of a piglet sculpted on it.

Scenes from the inner town (this page)*: the church of San Felice has a two-bell campanile; the streets around abound with interesting detail – a restaurant in the Via Gramsci, a fountain in the Via San Lino, and a wine shop in the Via Matteotti. The houses on the Via della Petraia* (opposite)*, near the Porta San Felice, cluster together in almost organic fashion.*

On the opposite side of the *piazza* access can be gained to the Duomo and to the Palazzo Vescovile, the former bishop's palace and home of the Museo d'Arte Sacra, one of the most remarkable institutions of Volterra. It contains a number of works of art, mainly drawn from local churches; notable among them are a gilded bronze crucifix, thought to be by Giambologna, and a fifteenth-century reliquary bust by Antonio del Pollaiuolo. The cathedral itself was consecrated in 1120, but much changed in the Pisan style in the mid thirteenth century, hence the marble decoration of the façade. The inside contains more treasures than can be enumerated here, but especially memorable is a fine tabernacle, sculpted by Mino da Fiesole; in a small chapel off the north aisle are two terracotta representations of the *Adoration of the Magi* and the *Nativity* by Luca and Andrea della Robbia, with frescoed backgrounds by Benozzo Gozzoli. An interesting older

High and precarious on the crumbling ridge, Volterra makes an impressive showing against the sky (overleaf)*.*

work is a gilded and painted wooden carving of the *Deposition from the Cross* by an anonymous Pisan sculptor. Much of the interior of the cathedral was remodelled in the later sixteenth century to designs by Leonardo Ricciarelli.

Completing the ensemble around the square of the Duomo is the octagonal baptistry, built in the late thirteenth century on the site of an ancient temple devoted to worship of the sun, and the fourteenth-century hospital of Santa Maria Maddalena. The former's greatest treasure is the old baptismal font by Andrea Sansovino.

In spite of its dramatic siting and its wealth of religious art and architecture, however, perhaps the essential flavour of Volterra is to be found in those streets where the finer *palazzi* of the town are located, in the Via Roma, for example, or the Via Ricciarelli, or the Via dei Sarti. Here, in the shadow of the imposing façades – like those of the tower houses of the Buomparenti or the sixteenth-century Palazzo Viti, attributed to Bartolomeo Ammannati – comes a sense of the fascinations and mysteries of this town, especially when the narrow streets and alleyways are enveloped in an early morning mist.

SOUTHERN TUSCANY

This is a land of pale-blue lakes and lagoons, perhaps best typified by the region known as the Maremma, a huge area with abundant wild-life, pine forests and a coastline which runs from Porto Ercole and Orbetello in the south to Follonica in the north. The dunes of the area are home to countless birds; notably rich in bird-life is the area around Orbetello which sits between two lagoons on a causeway linking the mainland with the Argentario promontory. Inland, southern Tuscany becomes mountainous and includes Monte Amiata, an extinct volcano which is the highest peak in Tuscany south of the Arno. In the east, the region is renowned for its hill-towns and thermal springs. To the north the area reaches Massa Marittima in the foot-hills of the Colline Metallifere (the 'metalliferous hills').

The various phases of Tuscan history are abundantly evident in all these places. Chiusi played a major role in Etruscan politics, being one of the twelve towns of the Confederation, and still retains its massive Etruscan necropolis. And its cathedral, though founded in the sixth century, incorporates Roman columns. The wars of the Middle Ages have left us the fortifications built by the Sienese at Massa Marittima. And at Orbetello there is a sixteenth-century powder works built by the Spanish occupation forces of Philip II.

Vertiginous steps lead down to the harbour at Porto Ercole.

Chianciano Terme

IN A REGION FAMOUS FOR its spas, Chianciano Terme is one of the most popular. Elegant spa buildings, dating mainly from the nineteen-thirties, fine parks, gardens and fountains cater for the thousands of visitors who flock to sample the waters in and out of season. The thermal springs have a long history; they were used by the Etruscans eight centuries before the Christian era, and the Romans (who called the town *Fontes Clusinae*) also enjoyed their therapeutic qualities. Four thermal establishments – Acqua Sillene, Acqua Santa, Acqua Sant'Elena and Acqua Fucoli – now treat rheumatism, disorders of the liver and bladder and even nervous afflictions, either by imbibing of the waters or bathing in them.

In addition to its modern spa buildings, Chianciano Terme has an impressive old town, which dominates the valley of the Chiana (left). The Porta Rivellini (above), seen here from the Viale Dante Alighieri, is one of the ancient gateways of the town.

*T*he main spa building (opposite) *of the Parco Acqua Santa dates from 1952, the work of architects Mario Marchi and Mario Loreti. Elsewhere in the surrounding park, those in search of cures indulge in traditional pleasures* (this page).

The picturesque and winding streets of the old town, like the Via delle Mura (right) and the Via A. Casini (opposite), give a good idea of the defensive siting of the place. The former leads round the remains of the old town wall from the Porta del Sole to the Porta Rivellini; the latter takes the visitor to the medieval Torre dell' Orologio (now restored). A pleasant, animated place, Chianciano Vecchia also takes pride in a vigorous market (below).

Other pleasant resort towns and villages lie to the north and south of Chianciano and its pleasant siting in the rolling hills of the Valdichiana: Sant'Albino, San Casciano dei Bagni, Sarteano (with a fourteenth-century Sienese fortress) and Cetona, founded by the Etruscans in the shade of Monte Cetona.

Closer by, adjoining the modern spa town, is medieval Chianciano Vecchia, which yields magnificent views over the valley of the Chiana. It has a number of important buildings, including a thirteenth-century Palazzo del Podestà, decorated with fifteenth- and sixteenth-century escutcheons, and a collegiate church, notable for its thirteenth-century portal. The eighteenth-century Palazzo dell'Arcipretura is now a museum of sacred art, providing a welcome alternative to the more modish pleasures of the spa. Important works in the collection include a thirteenth-century Florentine *St. John the Baptist*, a late-thirteenth-century

carving of the *Madonna and Child*, from the workshop of Arnolfo di Cambio, and a *Crucifixion* by a follower of Duccio di Buoninsegna. Another gem of the old town is the church of the Madonna della Rosa, a sixteenth-century delight in brick and stone. Just outside the village, and a wonderful place to review the historical presences of the place is an archaeological museum, the Museo Etrusco, in an old granary.

During the olive harvest the groves around the town become places of intense activity (this page). More tranquil is the grove surrounding the late-Renaissance church of the Madonna della Rosa (left), built in the form of a Greek cross in 1585 to the design of Baldassare Lanci.

Chiusi

The Piazza del Duomo (above) *is flanked by the cathedral, famous for its Roman pillars* (opposite)*, the episcopal palace and the Museo Nazionale Etrusco.*

SET ON A ROCKY SPUR amid olive groves and vineyards punctuated with the long skyward-pointing fingers of cypresses, Chiusi dominates the valley of the Chiana. Once a tributary of the Tiber, this river gave the town direct contact with Rome, under whose rule it fell in 296 B.C. and under whose guidance the present street pattern was established. But it is the presence of the Etruscans which most powerfully informs Chiusi and its immediate surroundings.

Its most famous king was Lars Porsena, who had the temerity to attack Rome in 507 B.C., only to be repelled by Horatius, as celebrated in Lord Macaulay's much-quoted poem. According to Pliny, the king is buried in the Poggio Gaiella, a hill to the north of the town, but the exact whereabouts of the tomb remains unknown. The Museo Nazionale Etrusco, founded in 1871, is a major celebration of Chiusi's ancient past. There are numerous artefacts excavated nearby in its display,

including sarcophagi and urns which reveal the fascination with death of the original inhabitants of this ancient land. And on the route to the town's lake, the Lago di Chiusi (to the north and once part of an extensive marsh), are a number of fine tombs with wall-paintings of Etruscan life, some of which can be visited.

Close to the Museo Etrusco, in the centre of the town, is the major monument of Christian-era Chiusi – the Duomo, the sixth-century cathedral of San Secondiano. The church building, set in a pleasant arcaded square, replaced an earlier pagan temple, and

was itself substantially rebuilt in the thirteenth century and latterly restored at the end of the nineteenth. Evidence of its early origins is, however, still abundant; the roof of the nave, for instance, is partly supported by eighteen varied Roman columns taken from other sites. Later additions include an alabaster font with a figure of St. John the Baptist, probably by a follower of Andrea Sansovino, and what look like antique mosaics but are in fact paintings dating from the nineteenth-century restoration. Above the high altar is a monument to St. Mustiola, patron saint of Chiusi; she was flogged to death in A.D. 274 on the orders of the

Once an important Etruscan town, Chiusi is notable for its wealth of remains of that mysterious people, both in the public park (below) *and in the national museum* (opposite).

Another important collection in Chiusi is that of illuminated music manuscripts, housed in the cathedral museum; this antiphonary (above) *was illuminated in 1467 by Liberale da Verona. Following the convention of plainsong, the music has four lines to contain the notes.*

HOC PERISTYLIVM
PETRVS NARDI DEI
ÆRE SVO F. F.
MCMI

*A*nother attraction for visitors to Chiusi are the lakes
to the north, the Lago di Chiusi (these pages) *and
the smaller Lago di Montepulciano. Once part of an
extensive marsh, both are famous for their variety of
bird- and plant-life.*

Imperial commander of the region, during a campaign of persecution of the Christian community. The campanile stands apart from the cathedral, covering an immense Roman cistern. In the cathedral's museum is an important collection of illuminated music manuscripts. Other notable churches in Chiusi are the fourteenth-century San Lorenzo and the thirteenth-century Santa Maria della Misericordia.

Apart from the obvious nearby places to visit – Chianciano Terme, Sarteano and Cetona – San Casciano dei Bagni, another spa town, offers several delights. As well as the hot springs, which have been in use since Roman times, there is a Gothic castle and the exquisite collegiate church of San Leonardo. A thirteenth- to fourteenth-century structure, its high altarpiece (late fifteenth-century) by Pietro di Francesco Orioli represents the *Coronation of the Virgin*. And surrounding the town is countryside which is the quintessence of Tuscany: vineyards and forested hills.

Although a fitting end-note to a description of Chiusi may be a photograph of Etruscan remains (below), thought should be spared for the glories of the surrounding countryside – here, the wooded hills around San Casciano dei Bagni (left).

Massa Marittima

The magnificent cathedral (opposite), finished in 1314, is dedicated to St. Cerbone, the patron saint of the town. Siena's presence is expressed in a carving of a wolf, the city emblem, on the Palazzo Comunale (right). There is more of the medieval town in the Via Ximenes – the Palazzo dell' Abbondanza (below).

THIS ENTERTAININGLY COMPLEX town lies on an incline of the Colline Metallifere (the 'metalliferous hills'), dominating the Tuscan Maremma, the 'land by the sea'. It is hardly surprising, therefore, that Massa Marittima flourished as a mining town in the Middle Ages, deriving its wealth from the silver, copper and lead ore deposits in the hills. The high point of its economic well-being came in the early thirteenth century, when it declared itself a republic. Nearly a century later it issued its own currency, before falling to the Sienese in 1335. Later, malaria and the plague took their toll of the population and the mines went into decline. Only

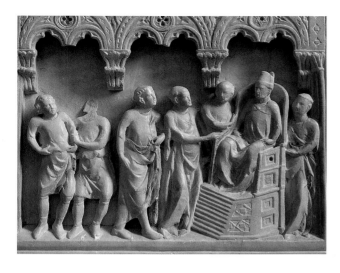

when the coastal marshes which harboured the malaria-carrying mosquitoes were drained did Massa Marittima start to regain its prosperity, a process of recovery helped by the reopening of the mines around 1830.

There are two distinct parts to the town: the lower Città Vecchia and the upper Città Nuova. The former is centred on the wide and sloping Piazza Garibaldi, home to the magnificent cathedral and the Palazzo del Podestà, both architectural treasures dating from Massa Marittima's golden age. Dedicated to St. Cerbone, patron saint of the town, the imposing Romanesque-Gothic Duomo rises from a majestic flight of steps. Built mostly in the thirteenth century and finished around 1314, it has a lower façade of seven blind arches supporting an upper part of arches and capitals in the Pisan Gothic style. Above the main door are carvings depicting scenes from the life of St. Cerbone, once

condemned to be torn apart by bears but, having miraculously survived, then destined to become Bishop of Populonia, eventually dying peacefully in Elba in 580. Fourteenth-century stained-glass in the rose-window also portrays an incident from the saint's life; here, he is kneeling before Pope Virgilius who had summoned the bishop to Rome to explain his practice of celebrating Mass before dawn, much disliked by the congregation of Populonia. Next to the main building of the cathedral rises the Gothic campanile, added around 1400.

Inside is a magnificent travertine font carved by Giroldo da Como in 1267 with scenes from the life of John the Baptist; the mid-fifteenth-century cover has carvings of the Twelve Apostles. In a subsidiary chapel is one of the great art treasures of the cathedral: a 1316 painting of the *Madonna delle Grazie*, possibly by Duccio di Buoninsegna or Simone Martini. Behind

*M*assa Marittima cathedral contains some magnificent treasures: its rectangular font (opposite), *with thirteenth-century reliefs of scenes of St. John the Baptist carved by Giroldo da Como and of Jesus blessing the baptized, and the fifteenth-century tabernacle; the 1324 marble Arca di San Cerbone by Goro di Gregorio* (top left); *an eleventh-century wooden panel of the Apostles; a Byzantine-style* Crucifixion (above) *by Segna di Bonaventura.*

*T*he sumptuous façade of the Duomo (opposite) is embellished with white, red and green marble. Seven blind arches support two further tiers of arches, and from each storey peer out lions. In contrast, the cloister of Sant' Agostino (above right) in the Città Nuova appears a place of retiring calm. On the Piazza Garibaldi stands the thirteenth-century Palazzo del Podestà (below right); it now serves as the town's archaeological museum and art gallery. The façade is decorated with the coats of arms of the rulers of Massa Marittima between 1426 and 1633.

The town at play and at prayer: drums outside the former church of San Pietro all' Orto (below); the Palm Sunday procession (right and right below); the arduous climb up the Via Moncini, which leads from the cathedral to the Porta alle Sicili (opposite).

the high altar, itself notable for a wooden *Crucifixion* by Giovanni Pisano, is a series of eight bas-reliefs of 1324, known as the Arca di San Cerbone, by the Sienese sculptor Goro di Gregorio.

Just to the west of the cathedral on the Piazza Garibaldi is Massa Marittima's other major architectural legacy from the thirteenth century: the Palazzo del Podestà, home to the local archaeological collection and at least one considerable work of art. This is the *Maestà* painted by Ambrogio Lorenzetti *c.* 1330, showing the Madonna and Child. In one corner is a representation of St. Cerbone with geese, an allusion to the saint's journey to Rome to meet Pope Virgilius – the geese were intended as a gift. The façade of the palace is

adorned with the coats of arms of the governers of Massa Marittima from 1426 to 1633. On the same *piazza* is the Palazzo Comunale, a complex of varying dates, from a thirteenth-century tower to a sixteenth-century interior.

The upper part of the town has a very different feel to it, being rectilinear in plan and retaining a substantial part of the fortifications introduced by the Sienese after their capture of Massa Marittima in the fourteenth century. Reached by way of the Via Moncini, most of the finer buildings cluster around the Piazza Matteotti. These include the thirteenth-century Torre del Candeliere, linked by an arch to the Porta alle Silici, part of the curtain wall of the fortress built by the Sienese. In the vicinity, too, is thirteenth-century San Francesco, once truncated after a landslide. And a fitting conclusion to a visit to the upper town is a walk along the Corsa A. Diaz to the half-Romanesque, half-Gothic church of Sant'Agostino.

The thirteenth-century Romanesque-Gothic church of San Francesco (left) *has been substantially reconstructed over the centuries, but still retains its original polygonal apse. Along the Via dei Bastioni remain the traces of the occupying Sienese in the form of their defensive walls* (below).

Orbetello

THE MOST POTENT HISTORICAL legacy left to Orbetello is announced immediately on the town gate in the form of the arms of Philip II of Spain. The latter entered into an alliance with Cosimo I of Florence in 1557 to end Sienese rule in the region; the Spanish retained the right to garrison the coastal area (the *Stato dei Presidi*), building the ramparts and gates which remain the dominant features of the town. Their arms manufactory and arsenal, the Polveriera Guzman, suvives as one of its finest buildings. Later, the town passed through Austrian and French hands, eventually becoming part of Napoleon's empire before incorporation into the Grand Duchy of Tuscany in 1815.

There is evidence in Orbetello of a much earlier history of importance; indeed, the town may very well

M onte Argentario, cloud-laden, looms across the lagoon of Orbetello (opposite)*; an interesting detail in the lagoon is this former windmill* (above)*. The Spanish legacy is given a very solid-looking expression in the Porta Medina Coeli* (right)*.

In the Piazza Garibaldi rises the Palazzo del Governatore, the palace of the Spanish governor, with its bust of Garibaldi (above).

have been the principal port of the Etruscan federation. An Etruscan wall still lines part of the canal which runs from above the Piazza del Popolo to link the town's two lagoons. In the Palazzo della Pretura in the Via Ricasoli is a collection of Etruscan and Roman remains discovered on sites in and around the town, including remarkable tufa sphinxes from the seventh and sixth centuries B.C.

Though an appealing place, especially around the palm-planted waterfront, Orbetello does not have a large number of architecturally dramatic buildings. Notable, however, is the exquisite little Gothic cathedral, dedicated to Santa Maria Assunta and begun in 1376. Especially delightful are its façade, with the bust of St. Biagio, and a rose-window; these were happily preserved in the major rebuilding of the mid seven-

teenth century. Inside, the saint is further celebrated in a chapel dedicated to him; its Romanesque altar is carved with the forms of peacocks and branches of vines. There is also a fresco depicting Pope Pius XII.

It is really because of its surroundings and its extraordinary siting between the mainland and the Argentario peninsula that Orbetello proves such a fascinating place to visit. In summer the promontory is a favourite Tuscan holiday and excursion spot, especially the peak of Monte Argentario itself, which offers views as far as Corsica on fine days. The lagoons are home to thousands of birds, including rare species, and to a wildlife reserve planted with oaks and pines and teeming with pheasants and fallow deer.

South of Orbetello and close to the resort of Ansedonia are the ruins of the Roman town of Cosa,

The Piazza Garibaldi is also the town centre for animated conversation or the quiet perusal of a newspaper (below *and* foot of page). *The piazza and that of the cathdral are connected by the Via Solferino. When the cathedral, dedicated to Santa Maria Assunta, was rebuilt in 1660, the Gothic façade and doorways were retained* (left).

The lagoon of Orbetello, seen here from the Via Mura di Levante (above) *is famous for the variety and extent of its bird-life.*

an important and thriving community about the time of the birth of Christ. There are a number of surviving walls, a forum, the remains of two temples, mosaics and wall-paintings. Another nature reserve close by is the Lago di Burano, which is in fact a lagoon. Reached along the beach from Ansedonia, it is famous for the variety of its surrounding vegetation and the richness

of its bird-life. Together with Orbetello's lagoon, this stretch of coast is generally agreed to be the most important wetland reserve of the west of the Italian peninsula.

Another attractive location to the south of the lagoon is the ancient town of Porto Ercole, compact and intimate and now a flourishing resort. It was

founded in the Etruscan era, thrived under the Romans but went into decline because of the attentions of local pirates. During the Spanish era, however, it revived again and still owes its present form to the building which took place in the sixteenth century, much of it with a military purpose. No fewer than three fortresses date from that time; two face each

One example of the bird-life of this coast: a stork-like ibis perches serenely on a venerable jetty (above). Another aspect of this coast is the high number of important archaeological sites, including Cosa (Roman Portus Cosanus) (top), where walls, a forum and the remains of two temples have been excavated.

*W*herever one looks along this coastline, whether in the details of towns or out to sea, there is always something of fascination: the graceful harbour at Porto Ercole (opposite); the sandy spit of the Tombolo di Giannella (above); a plaque on Orbetello's Palazzo Comunale (right); the setting sun across the lagoon (overleaf).

other across the harbour and a third one rises above the town on the south side. Even the ruined Rocca, though originally dating from the thirteenth century, was substantially rebuilt in the sixteenth. In the following century Porto Ercole staked another claim to fame, for it was close to here that the painter Caravaggio died, possibly of malaria, possibly of sunstroke, in 1610. He was buried in the local parish church of Sant'Erasmo; there is a memorial to him in the form of a plaque on the gateway to the old town.

Pontrémoli

Barga

PISTOIA
Pescia • • Montecatini
Terme
■ PRATO
■ LUCCA
SERCHIO

Fiesole
FLORENCE ■

PISA ■
San
Miniato
Impruneta
San Casciano
in Val di Pesa
ELSA
Certaldo

LIVORNO ■

VOLTERRA ■
Colle di
Val d'Elsa
Monteriggioni
■ SIENA
CECINA

Bibbiena

Sansepolcro •

■ AREZZO

Castiglion
• Fiorentino
CORTONA ■

T U S C A N Y

Tyrrhenian

MASSA MARITTIMA
■

Montepulciano

Chianciano
Terme •
• Chiusi

ARNO

OMBRONE

GROSSETO
■

S e a

ELBA

ALBEGNA

ORVIETO ■

N

| 0 | 5 | 10 | 20 | 30 | 40 km |

| 0 | 5 | 10 | 20 | 30 miles |

ORBETELLO
■

A Travellers' Guide

While every effort has been made to ensure that the information given in the following entries is correct, the author and the publisher cannot be held responsible for any inadvertent inaccuracies. Opening dates and times of local attractions change seasonally and sometimes alter from year to year; it is always advisable to check with the venue or the nearest tourist information office in advance.

TOURIST BOARDS

Italian State Tourist Board, Great Britain and Ireland, 1 Princes Street, London WIR 8AY; tel. (020) 7408 1254.

Italian Government Travel Office, Street 1565, 6th Avenue, New York 10111 630; tel. (212) 245 4822.

Tuscan Regional State Tourist Office in Florence, Via di Novoli 26, Firenze; tel. (055) 438 2111.

Italian Government Travel Office, Canada, Quebec Store, 1 Place Ville-Marie, Suite 1914, Montreal H3B 2C3; tel. (514) 866 7676.

NORTHERN TUSCANY

Barga

Sights & Events
Opera festival, July and August.

Where to Stay
ALPINO, Via G. Pascoli 41; tel. (0583) 723336.

LA PERGOLA, Via Sant' Antonio 46; tel. (0583) 711239.

VILLA LIBANO, Via del Sasso 6; tel. (0583) 723774.

Information
Piazza Angelico; tel. (0583) 723499.

Bibbiena

Sights & Events
Bello Ballo, Shrove Tuesday celebrations dating back to the fourteenth century.

Where to Stay
BROGI; tel. (0575) 536222.

Where to Eat
MON AMI.

Information
Via Berni 25; tel. (0575) 593098.

Fiesole

Sights & Events
Museo Bandini, Via Dupré; open 10.00–12.00 and 14.00–17.00; Closed 18.00 in summer, and on the first Tuesday of each month; superb della Robbia terracottas; Tuscan paintings, the finest from the fifteenth and sixteenth centuries.

Roman theatre, excavations and museum; open 09.00–19.00 in summer, 09.00–16.00 in winter; closed the first Tuesday of each month; tel. (055) 59477.

Where to Stay
VILLA AURORA, Piazza Mino 39; tel. (055) 59100.

VILLA BONELLI, Via Poeti 1–3; tel. (055) 59513.

BENCISTÀ, Via Benedetto da Maiano 4; tel. (055) 59163.

VILLA SAN MICHELE, Via Doccia 4;
tel. (055) 59451.

CAMPING PANORAMICO, Via Peramonda;
tel. (055) 599069.

Information
Piazza Mino da Fiesole 37;
tel. (055) 598720.

Impruneta

Sights & Events
Horse and mule fair, dedicated to St. Luke,
15–18 October.

Wine harvest festival .

Church treasury; open summer, Thurs. and Fri.
10.00–13.00, Sat. and Sun. 10.00–13.00, 16.00–19.30;
winter Fri. 10.00–13.00, Sat. 15.00–18.30,
Sun. 10.00–13.00, 15.00–18.30.

Where to Stay
ALBERGO RISTORANTE BELLAVISTA,
Piazza della Croce 2;
tel. (055) 2011083.

Where to Eat
I TRE PINA, Pozzolatico (near Impruneta).

Information
Via Mazzini 1;
tel. (055) 2313729.

Monsummano Terme

Sights & Events
Grotta Giusti, cave;
tel. (0572) 51165.

Where to Stay
GROTTA GIUSTI, Via Grotta Giusti;
tel. (0572) 51165.

Montecatini Terme

Thermal Establishments
Terme Tettuccio, Viale Verdi;
tel. (0572) 778501.

Terme La Salute, Via della Salute;
tel. (0572) 778571

Terme Leopoldine, Viale Verdi;
tel. (0572) 778551.

Terme Torretta, Via Baragiola;
tel. (0572) 778541.

Terme Redi, Viale Bicchiera;
tel. (0572) 778531.

Terme Excelsior, Viale Verdi;
tel. (0572) 778511.

Terme Tamerici, Viale Tamerici;
tel. (0572) 778561.

Tickets for all the thermal establishments from the
Società delle Terme, Viale Verdi 41;
tel. (0572) 778451.

Sights & Events
Accademia d'Arte, Viale A. Diaz; open every day
except Monday in summer, 16.00–19.30, every day
except Mondays and Saturdays in winter, 15.00–18.00.

Sesina Hippodrome, with races from spring to autumn.

La Toretta, tennis club.

Medici Villa , Poggio a Caiano; only the gardens are
open to visitors; closed the 2nd and 3rd Monday of
each month.

Where to Stay
Some 220 establishments, including
the GRAND HOTEL E LA PACE, Corso Roma 12;
tel. (0572) 75801.

Information
Viale Verdi 66;
tel. (0572) 772244.

Pescia

Sights & Events
Museo Civico, Piazza Santo Stefano; with medieval
and Renaissance paintings; open Wed., Fri., Sat.,
10.00–13.00; Thurs., 16.00–18.00.

Flower Biennale, in September of even numbered
years.

Where to Stay
VILLA DELLE ROSE, Via del Castellare;
tel. (0572) 451301.

Where to Eat
CECCO, Via Forti 84;
tel. (0572) 477955.

La Buca, Piazza Mazzini 4;
tel. (0572) 477339.

Information
As for Montecatini Terme.

Pontrémoli

Sights & Events
Castello del Piagnaro, at the heart of the medieval town, displays pre-Etruscan archaeological finds from the region; open except Mondays, 09.00–12.00 and 16.00–19.00 in summer, otherwise 09.00–12.00 and 14.00–17.00.

Where to Stay
Napoleon, Piazza Italia 2;
tel. (0187) 830544.

Where to Eat
Da Bussè, Piazza Duomo 9;
tel. (0187) 831371.

Bacciottini, Via Ricci Armani;
tel. (0187) 830120.

Information
Piazza Municipio;
tel. (0187) 831180.

San Casciano in Val di Pesa

Sights & Events
Museo di Arte Sacra, church of Santa Maria del Gesù; open Saturdays, 16.30–19.00, and Sundays, 10.00–12.30 and 16.00–19.00.

Where to Stay
L'Antica Posta, Piazza Zannoni 1;
tel. (055) 822313.

Where to Eat
Cantinetta del Nonno, Via IV Novembre 18;
tel. (055) 820570.

Da Nello, Via IV Novembre 64;
tel. (055) 820163.

Information
Local tourist office;
tel. (055) 8229558.

San Miniato

Sights & Events
Museo Diocesano d'Arte Sacra; open except Monday 09.00–12.30 and 15.00–18.30; in winter open only Saturdays and Sundays.

National kite-flying festival, first Sunday after Easter.

Drama festival, end of July.

Religious manifestations, Piazza del Duomo, August.

Palio di San Rocco, 16 August.

White truffle fair, end of November.

Where to Stay
Miravalle, Prato del Duomo 3;
tel. (0571) 418075.

Where to Eat
Antico Bar Trattoria, Via 4 Novembre;
tel. (0571) 400889.

Information
Piazza del Popolo 3;
tel. (0571) 42745.

Sansepolcro

Sights & Events
Museo Civico, Palazzo Comunale, Via Aggiunti 65; dates from the fifteenth century, with two works by Piero della Francesca; open 09.00–13.00 and 14.30–18.00 except for 1 January, 1 May, 15 August and 25 December.

Palio della Balestra, archery contest with the crossbowmen of Gubbio; 2nd Sunday in September; parades of citizens in costumes inspired by the works of Piero della Francesca.

Where to Stay
Fiorentino, Via Luca Pacioli 60;
tel. (0575) 740350.

Where to Eat
Al Coccio, Via Aggiunti 83;
tel. (0575) 749962.

Information
Piazza Garibaldi 2;
tel. (0575) 740536.

CENTRAL TUSCANY

Castiglion Fiorentino

Sights & Events
Palio dei Rioni, 3rd Sunday in June.

Where to Stay
Villa Schiatti, Via Montecchio 131, Montecchio Vesponi;
tel. (0575) 651481.

Where to Eat
Relais San Pietro, Polvano;
tel. (0575) 650100.

Information
Piazza Risorgimento 116, Arezzo;
tel. (0575) 23952.

Certaldo

Sights & Events
Palazzo Pretorio; open summer 09.30–12.30, 16.30–19.30; winter 10.00–12.00, 15.00–18.00.

Boccaccio house, Via Giovanni Boccaccio; open daily 09.00–12.00, 15.00–18.00;
tel. (0571) 664208.

Meracantia (theatre festival), last week of July.

Settembre Certaldese, music and theatre festival, September.

Where to Stay
Il Castello, Via della Rena 6;
tel. (0571) 668250.

Osteria del Vicario, Via Rivellino 3;
tel. (0571) 668228.

Casa al Cantone, Via Boccaccio 2;
tel. (0571) 667322.

Where to Eat
Il Castello (see above).

Osteria del Vicario (see above).

Information
Via Boccaccio 16;
tel. (0571) 664944.

Colle di Val d'Elsa

Sights & Events
Craft fair, September.

Where to Stay
Villa Belvedere, eighteenth-century villa just outside the town;
tel. (0577) 920966.

Hotel Arnolfo, Via Campana 8;
tel. (0577) 922020.

La Vecchia Cartiera, Via Oberdan 5/9;
tel. (0577) 921107.

Where to Eat
Osteria del Vicario (see above under *Certaldo*)

Information
Via Campana 43;
tel. (0577) 922791.

Montepulciano

Sights & Events
Museo Civico, Palazzo Neri-Orselli, Via Ricci 1; closed for restoration since 1997.

Feast of St. Agnese, with a fair, 1 May.

Cantiere Internazionale d'Arte (music, theatre and art), first half of August.

Bravio delle Botte (barrel-racing) through the streets with costumed participants, last Sunday in August.

Where to Stay
Panoramic, Via di Villa Bianca 8;
tel. (0578) 798398.

Il Marzocco, Piazza Savonarola 18;
tel. (0578) 757262.

Where to Eat
Porta di Bacco, Via di Gracciano 100;
tel. (0578) 716907.

Osteria dell' Acquacheta, Via del Teatro 22;
tel. (0578) 758443.

Information
Via Ricci 9;
tel. (0578) 758687.

Monteriggioni

Where to Stay
Hotel Monteriggioni, Castello di Monteriggioni 4;
tel. (0577) 305009.

Where to Eat
RESIDENCE SAN LUIGI, Strove;
tel. (0577) 301055.

IL POZZO, Piazza Roma 2;
tel. (0577) 304127.

LA CASALTA, Strove;
tel. (0577) 301002.

Information
Largo Fontebranda 5;
tel. (0577) 30481.

Volterra

Sights & Events
Museo di Arte Sacra, Palazzo Vescovile, Via Roma;
open daily except Mondays.

Museo Etrusco Guarnacci, Via Don Minzoni 15;
contains superb Etruscan treasures; open summer
09.00–19.00, winter 09.00–14.00.

Palazzo dei Priori; open weekdays in summer
10.00–13.00, 15.00–16.00, winter 10.00–13.00.

Pinacoteca and *Museo Civico*, Palazzo Minucci-Solaini,
Via Sarti 1; open summer 09.00–19.00, winter
09.00–14.00.

Parco Archeologico Fiumi, Via di Castello.

Astiludio, flag-throwing processions 1st Sunday in
September.

Theatre festival, July.

Saturday market, on the Piazza dei Priori.

Where to Stay
NAZIONALE, Via dei Marchesi;
tel. (0588) 86284.

VILLA NENCINI, Borgo Santo Stefano 55;
tel. (0588) 86386.

HOTEL SAN LINO, Via San Lino 26;
tel. (0588) 85250.

ETRURIA, Via Matteotti 32;
tel. (0588) 87377.

Where to Eat
DA BADÒ, Borgo San Lazzaro 9;
tel. (0588) 86051.

IL POZZO DEGLI ETRUSCHI, Via delle Prigioni 28;
tel. (0588) 80608.

DA BEPPINO, Via delle Prigioni;
tel. (0588) 86051.

OSTERIA DEI POETI, Via Matteotti 55;
tel. (0588) 86029.

ETRURIA, Piazza dei Priori 8;
tel. (0588) 86064.

IL PORCELLINO, Vicolo delle Prigioni;
tel. (0588) 86392.

Information
Via G. Turazza 2;
tel. (0588) 86150.

SOUTHERN TUSCANY

Chianciano Terme

Sights & Events
International folklore festival, July.

Musical season, May to October.

Museo della Collegiata, Palazzo dell' Arcipretura;
open summer 10.00–12.00, 16.00–19.00.

Where to Stay
GRAND HOTEL, Piazza Italia 80;
tel. (0578) 63333.

EXCELSIOR, Viale Sant' Agnese 6;
tel. (0578) 64351.

MICHELANGELO, Via delle Piane 146;
tel. (0578) 64004.

PARK HOTEL, Via Roncacci 30;
tel. (0578) 63603.

RAFFAELLO, Via del Monti 3;
tel. (0578) 64923.

Where to Eat
CASANOVA, Strada della Vittoda 10;
tel. (0578) 60449.

CASALE, Via delle Valle Cavine 36;
tel. (0578) 30445.

Information
Piazza Italia 67;
tel. (0578) 63167.

Chiusi

Sights & Events
Museo Nazionale Etrusco, Piazza del Duomo, showing Etruscan jewels, funeral urns, sarcophagi and Etruscan black pottery; open summer 09.00–20.00 on weekdays, and public holidays 09.00–13.00; winter daily 09.00–14.00, and public holidays 09.00–13.00.

Where to Stay
La Sfinge Etrusca, Via Marconi 2;
tel. (0578) 20157.

I Longobardi, at the railway station, three kilometres south-east of the town;
tel. (0578) 20115.

Vannucci, Via Vanni 1, Città della Pieve;
tel. (0578) 28063.

Where to Eat
Zaira, Via Arunte 12;
tel. (0578) 20260.

Osteria La Solita Zuppa, Via Porsenna 21;
tel. (0578) 21006.

Information
Via Porsenna 16;
tel. (0578) 227667.

Massa Marittima

Sights & Events
Il Girifalco, cross-bow contest in medieval costume, 20 May or following Sunday, and 2nd Sunday of August.

Palazzo del Podestà, open every day except Monday, summer 10.00–12.30, 15.30–19.00; winter 10.00–12.30, 15.00–17.00.

Where to Stay
Duca del Mare, Piazza Dante Alighieri 1;
tel. (0566) 902284.

Il Girifalco, Via Massetana Nord 25;
tel. (0566) 902177.

Il Sole, Via della Libertà 43;
tel. (0566) 901971.

Where to Eat
Osteria Da Tronco, Vicolo Porto 5;
tel. (0566) 901991.

Trattoria Da Alberto, Parenti 35;
tel. (0566) 902093.

Pizzeria I Tre Archi, Piazza Garibaldi;
tel. (0566) 902274.

Information
Via Norma Parenti 22;
tel. (0566) 902756.

Orbetello

Sights & Events
Museo Civico, Via Ricasole 26, impressive display of Etruscan and Roman remains.

Laguna di Ponente, nature reserve;
tel. (0564) 854892.

Where to Stay
I Presidi,
Via Mura di Levante 34;
tel. (0564) 867601.

Touring, Via Mazzini 21;
tel. (0564) 867151.

Hotel Corallo, Via Paolieri 27;
tel. (0564) 870065.

Argentario International Camping Village, Torre Saline; tel. (0564) 870302.

Where to Eat
Da Egisto, Corso Italia 190;
tel. (0564) 967469.

Information
Piazza della Repubblica;
tel. (0564) 861226.

Select Bibliography

ANDERSON, Burton, *Vino, the Wines and Winemakers of Italy*, London, 1980

BENTLEY, James, *Tuscany*, London, 1987

BENTLEY, James, *The Most Beautiful Villages of Tuscany,* London and New York, 1985

BENTLEY, James, *Italy: the Hilltowns,* London, 1990

DICKENS, Charles, *Pictures from Italy,* London, 1848

Italie du nord et du centre, Les Guides Bleus, Paris, 1982

KEATES, Jonathan, *Tuscany,* London, 1988

LAWRENCE, D.H., *Etruscan Places,* London, 1932

LAWRENCE, D.H., *Flowery Tuscany*, London, 1950

MACADAM, Alta, *Blue Guide to Tuscany*, London, 1993

MASSON, Georgina, *Italian Villas and Palaces*, London, 1959

Toscana (4th ed.), Touring Club Italiano, Milan, 1974

Acknowledgments

Photographer's Acknowledgments

I could not have photographed this book without the aid of local tourist offices. I am particularly grateful to Daniela Cocchini of Massa Marittima, Ilaria Stefani of Barga and Roberta Vichi of Volterra, who all went out of their way to be helpful. Thanks are also due to Signora Monti of the Comune di Pescia, Dr Lotti of the Fiesole Musei, the director of the Etruscan Museum in Volterra and Signora Malespina of the Villa Garzoni. Among the many friendly, courteous but sadly anonymous people who helped I must single out the farmer who dug out my car from a roadside ditch in the mountains abouve Barga.
The pictures I dedicate with love to Helena, who introduced me to Tuscany and who held the fort during my long absences.

Publisher's Note

Sadly, the author of this book, James Bentley, died suddenly during the latter stages of its production. It was his wish, however, that the text should be dedicated to Audrey W. Bentley. He also wished to extend especial thanks for help to Eduardo Betti, Director of the Italian State Tourist Board in London.